AF412293

Juan Muñoz

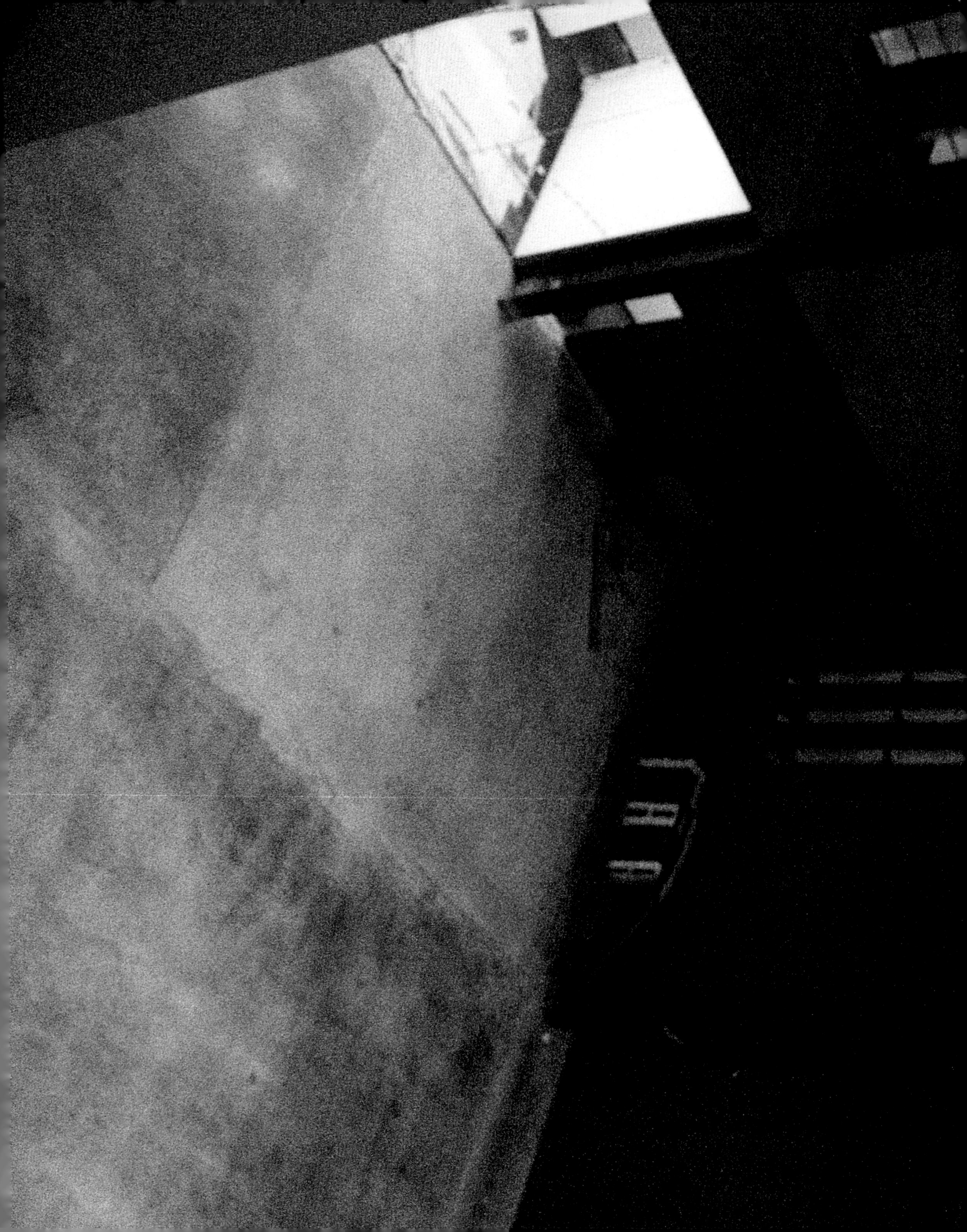

Juan Muñoz

Double Bind at Tate Modern

TATE PUBLISHING

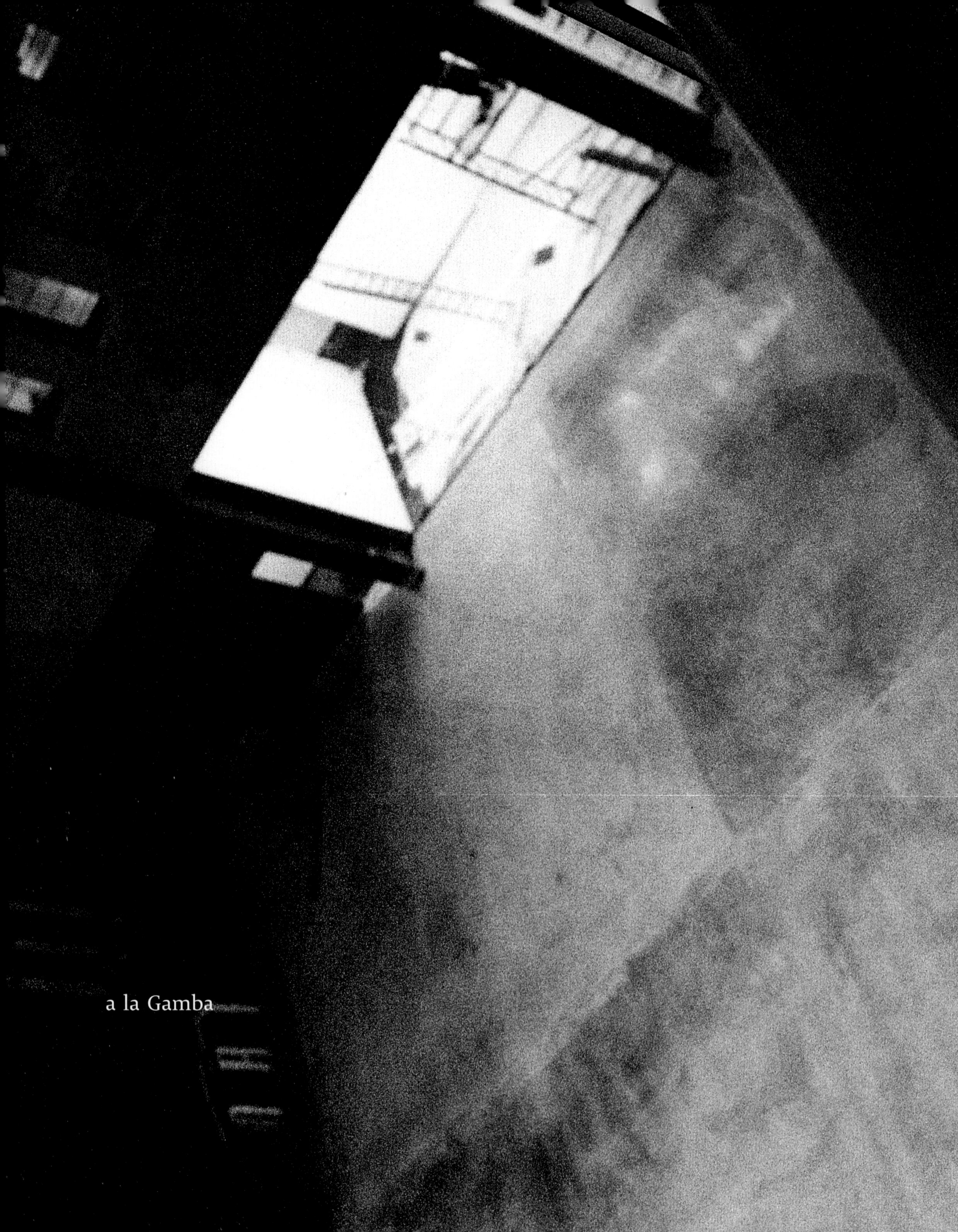
a la Gamba

Contents

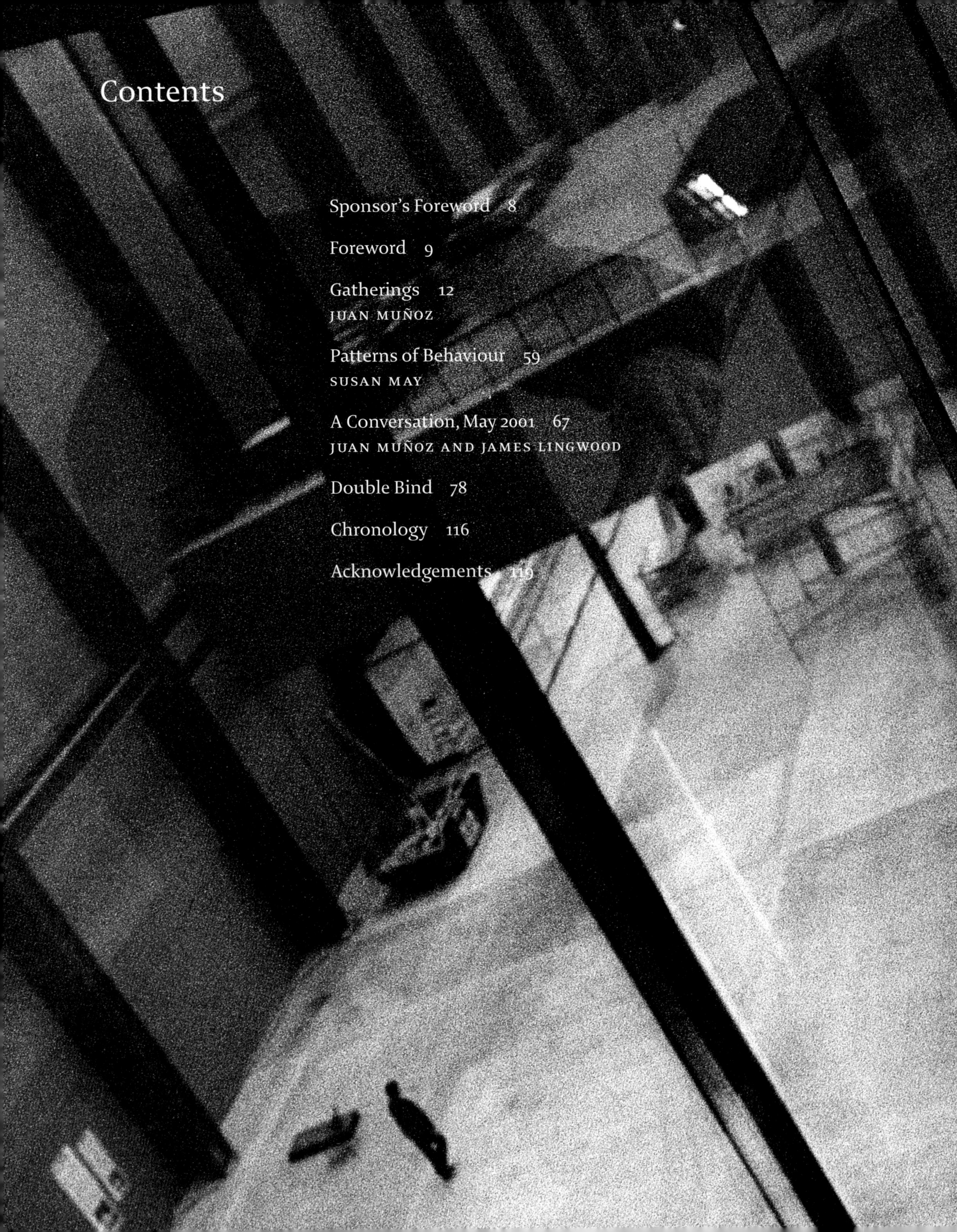

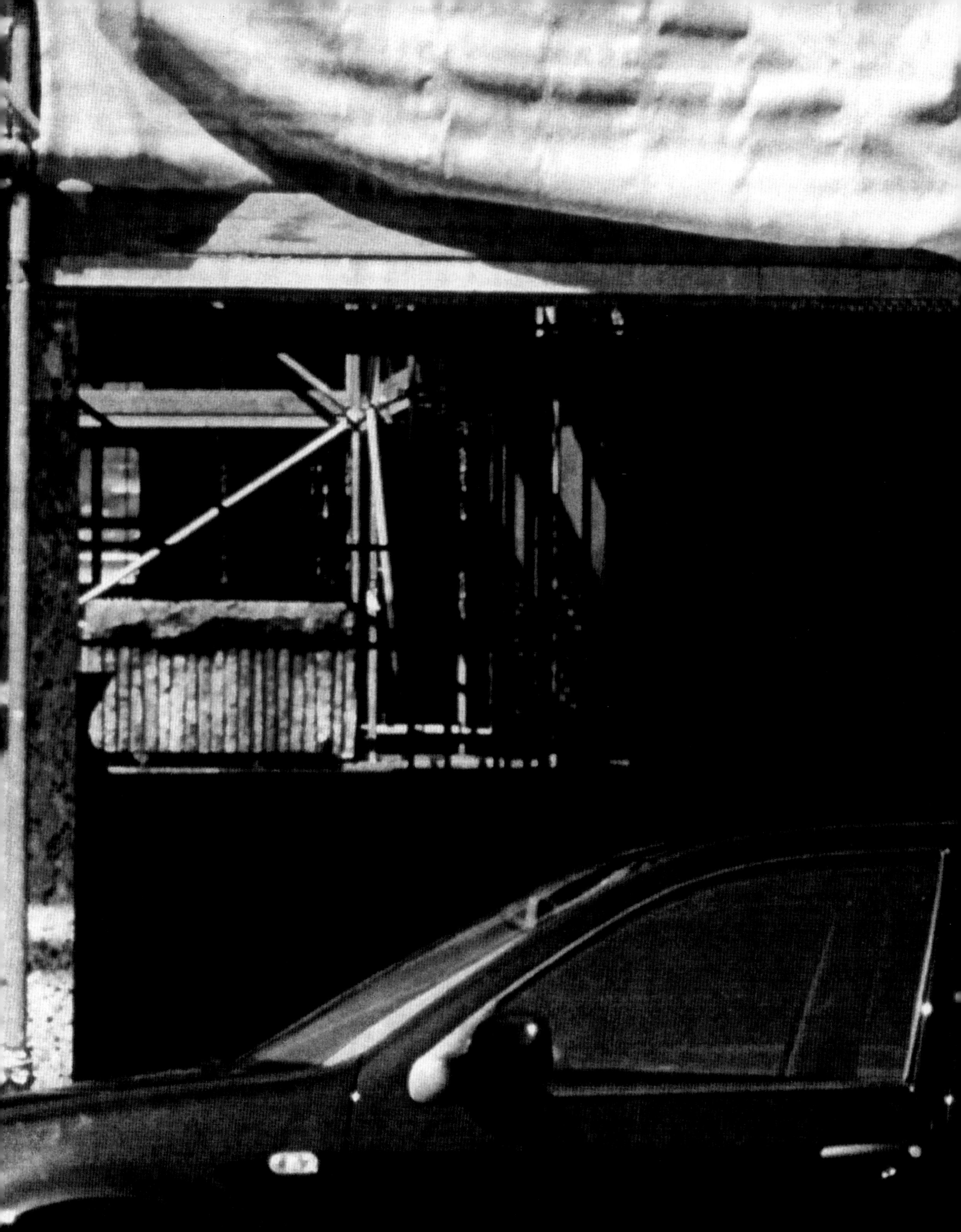

Sponsor's Foreword

The *Unilever Series* aims to bring the best in international creativity to Tate Modern's remarkable Turbine Hall. Undertaking the second commission in the series, Spanish artist Juan Muñoz has created an ambitious and highly imaginative work.

Muñoz's installation is stunning in its scope and ingenuity. Devised specifically to respond to the dimensions of the Turbine Hall, it playfully explores the shifts in scale between the building and the audience.

Unilever's support enables Tate Modern to commission and exhibit a new large-scale work each year until 2004. The inaugural work was created by one of the most influential artists of her generation, the French-born American sculptor Louise Bourgeois.

We are delighted that Juan Muñoz has responded so magnificently to the creative challenge of the Turbine Hall. We congratulate him on his achievement and hope that visitors to Tate Modern will share our admiration and enthusiasm for his work.

NIALL FITZGERALD
Chairman, Unilever

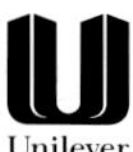

Unilever

Foreword

An unparalleled opportunity or a terrifying challenge? In February 2000 the sculptor Juan Muñoz was invited to make a work for Tate Modern's Turbine Hall, scene of the annual commission known as *The Unilever Series*. The space, which is over 150 metres long and 30 metres high, offers the rare opportunity to explore aspects of scale and distance, intimacy and monumentality. And yet, for the same reasons, it also poses very real challenges. The industrial architecture is powerful, even dominant, and the sheer number of people walking through the space on a busy day might be expected to render impossible any unique or singular meeting between viewer and artwork – the kind of encounter that lies at the heart of the art experience.

In responding to this challenge, Juan Muñoz has produced a work of incredible complexity, impact and beauty, and it has been an adventure and a pleasure to follow the creation of *Double Bind* at Tate Modern. Even though his visual strategies may be traceable to a pre-modern period, in particular the large-scale works of the Baroque, his approach is, if anything, rigorously contemporary. The allegory which Juan Muñoz places before the viewer, in a masterful choreography of space and object, leads not to higher and clarified insight, but rather to the realisation of the fundamental instability of language, and ultimately, the deceptiveness of the sign. In this way, the work of Juan Muñoz may be viewed as what the critic Paul de Man has called 'allegories of unreadability' – 'glorious, pleasurable and disquieting'.

I cannot thank Juan Muñoz enough for the privilege of working with him at Tate Modern, and for the experience he will give the millions of visitors who encounter this extraordinary work. We have greatly appreciated his intelligent approach to the commission, his creative solutions and ultimately his patience and good humour throughout. I would also like to extend my heartfelt thanks to Susan May, Curator at Tate Modern, who, with James Lingwood, has curated the exhibition and contributed to this book. In a project of this size and complexity, technical experts, fabricators and assistants play a critical role. Our warmest thanks go to David Scholefield, who led the technical production team, Neil Thomas, the project engineer, and Andrew McAlpine and Jim Morahan who created the design for the optical floor. Thanks also go to David Mason, Belinda Clisham, Anthony Joseph, Ana Fernández-Cid and Carolina Grau. In addition, I am indebted to the Tate Modern team who have helped to bring the project to fruition, particularly Adrian George, Assistant Curator, along with John Duffet, Phil Monk, Brian Gray, Sharon Hughes and Dennis Ahern.

For this book, Juan Muñoz has created an eloquent visual essay examining the genesis of the project. Featuring pages from his sketchbooks, architectural plans, found photographs and texts, all of which have a particular relevance for the artist, *Gatherings* offers an array of intriguing clues to the reading of *Double Bind*. We are grateful to Philip Lewis, who has designed this book in close collaboration with the artist; Mary Richards for editing the publication; and Sophie Lawrence who has skilfully overseen its production.

An experience like this cannot be offered in the absence of substantial financial support. Juan Muñoz's *Double Bind* is the second project in *The Unilever Series*, a series of commissions for the Turbine Hall at Tate Modern supported by Unilever. Our warmest thanks to the Chairman of Unilever, Niall FitzGerald, for his early commitment to Tate Modern and its audience.

LARS NITTVE
Director, Tate Modern

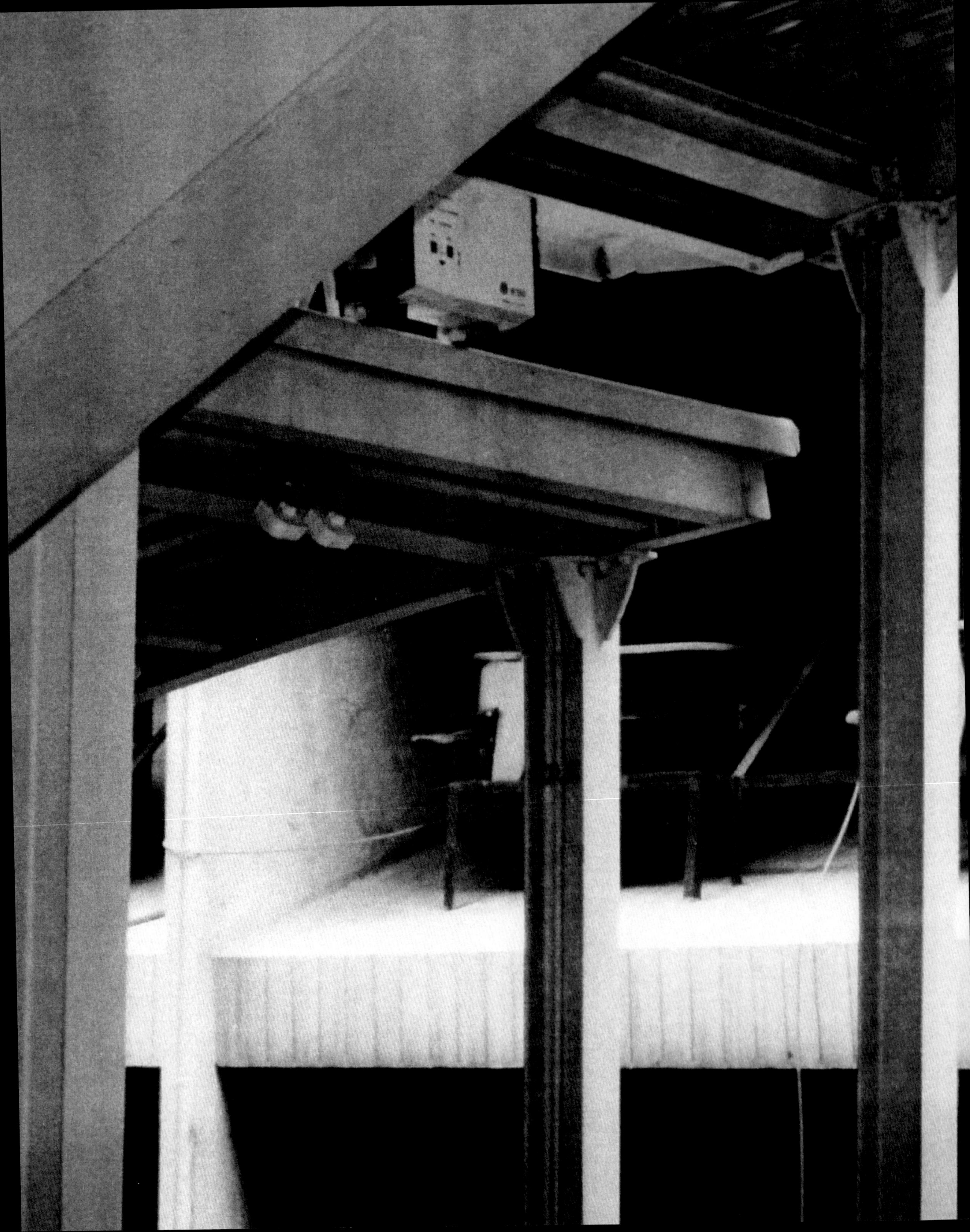

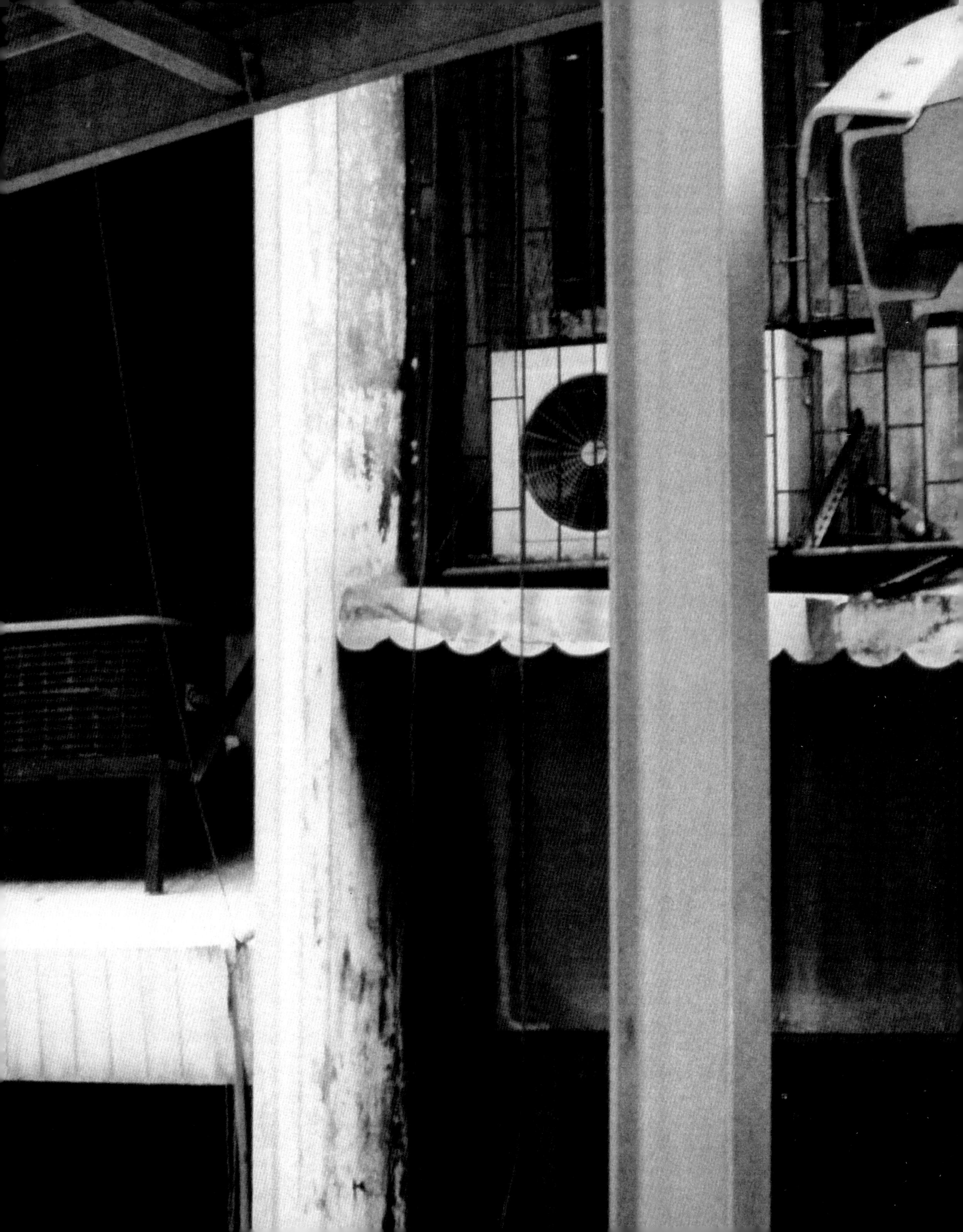

Gatherings

NOTES, DRAWINGS, PHOTOGRAPHS

20.03.00 | 03.06.01

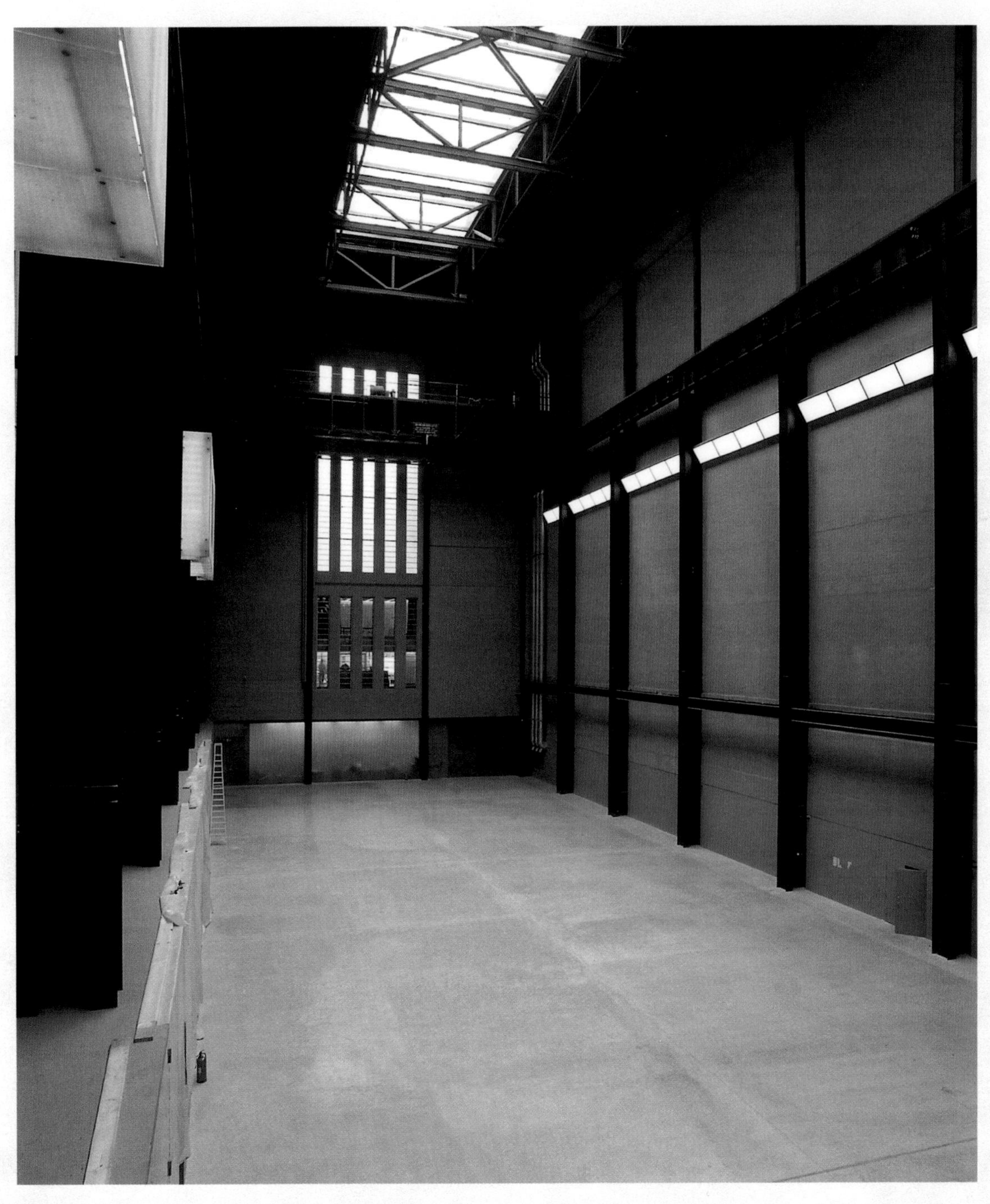

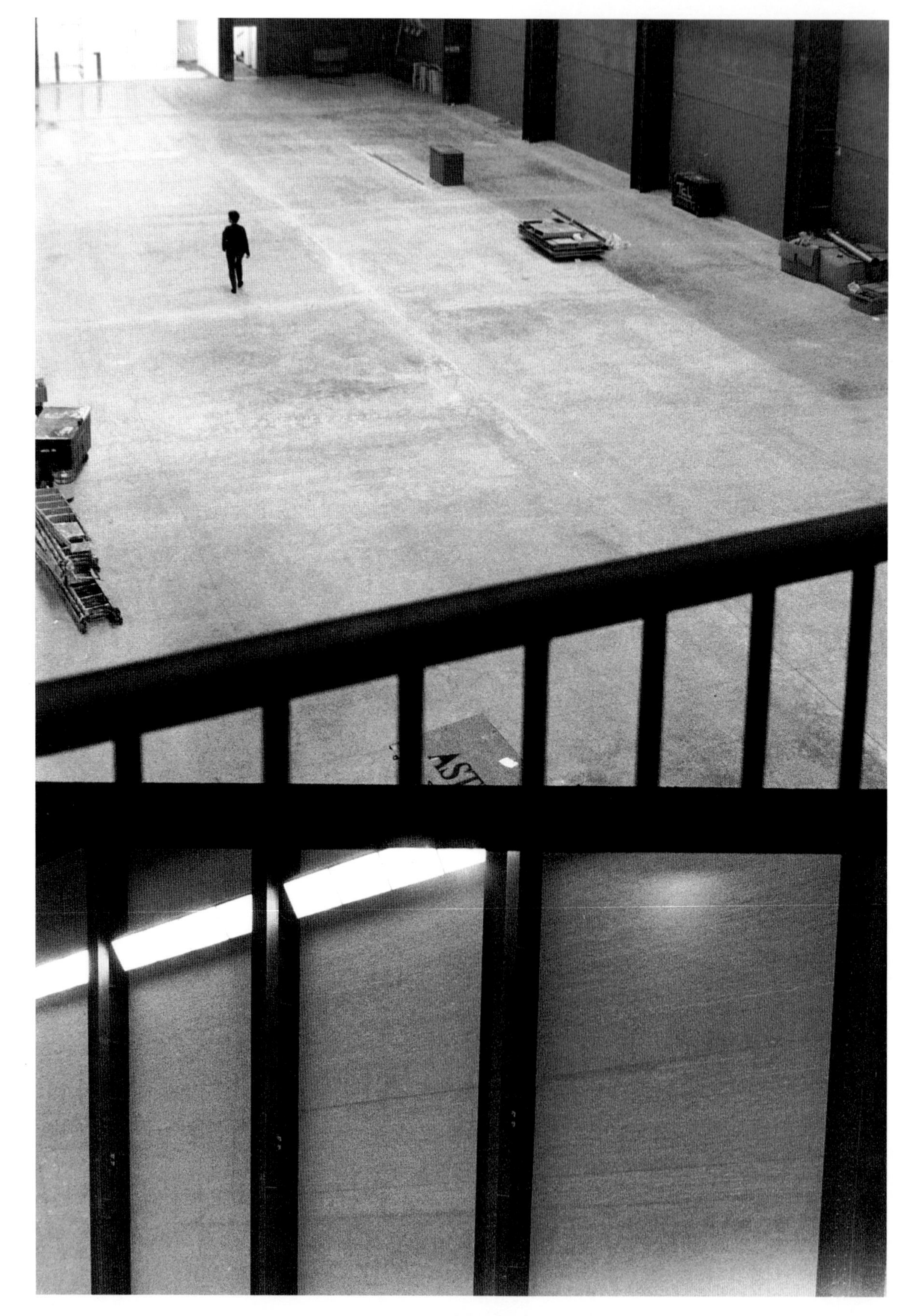

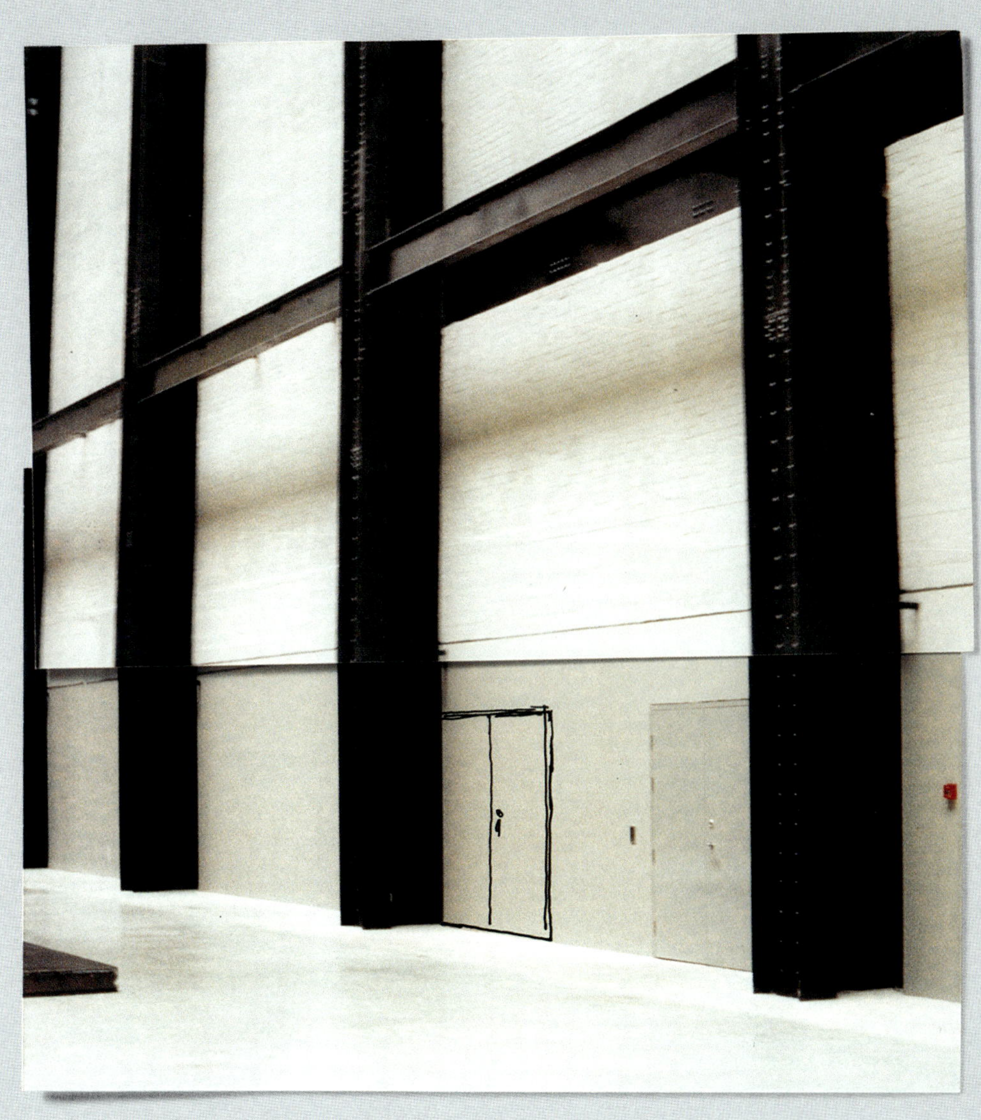

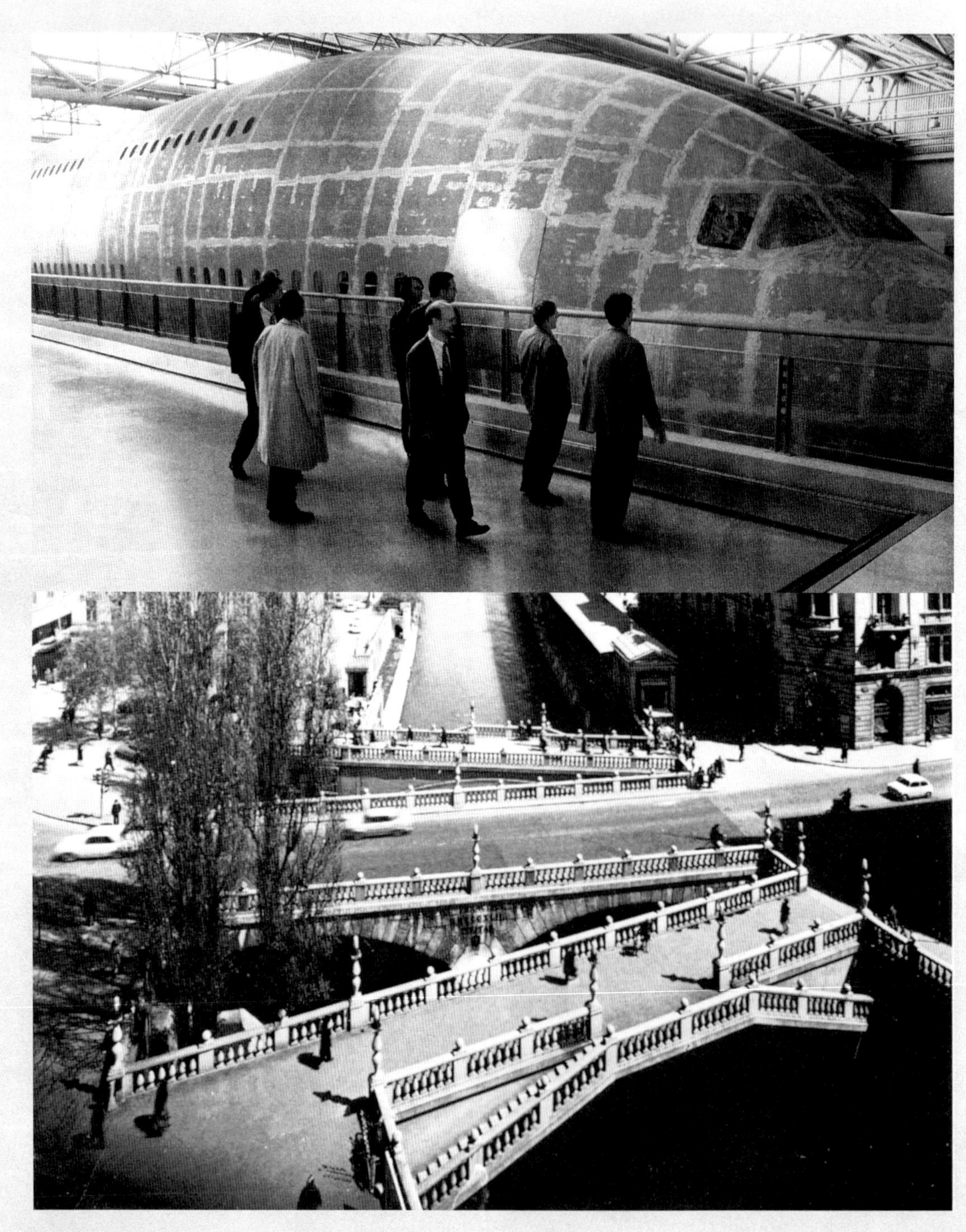

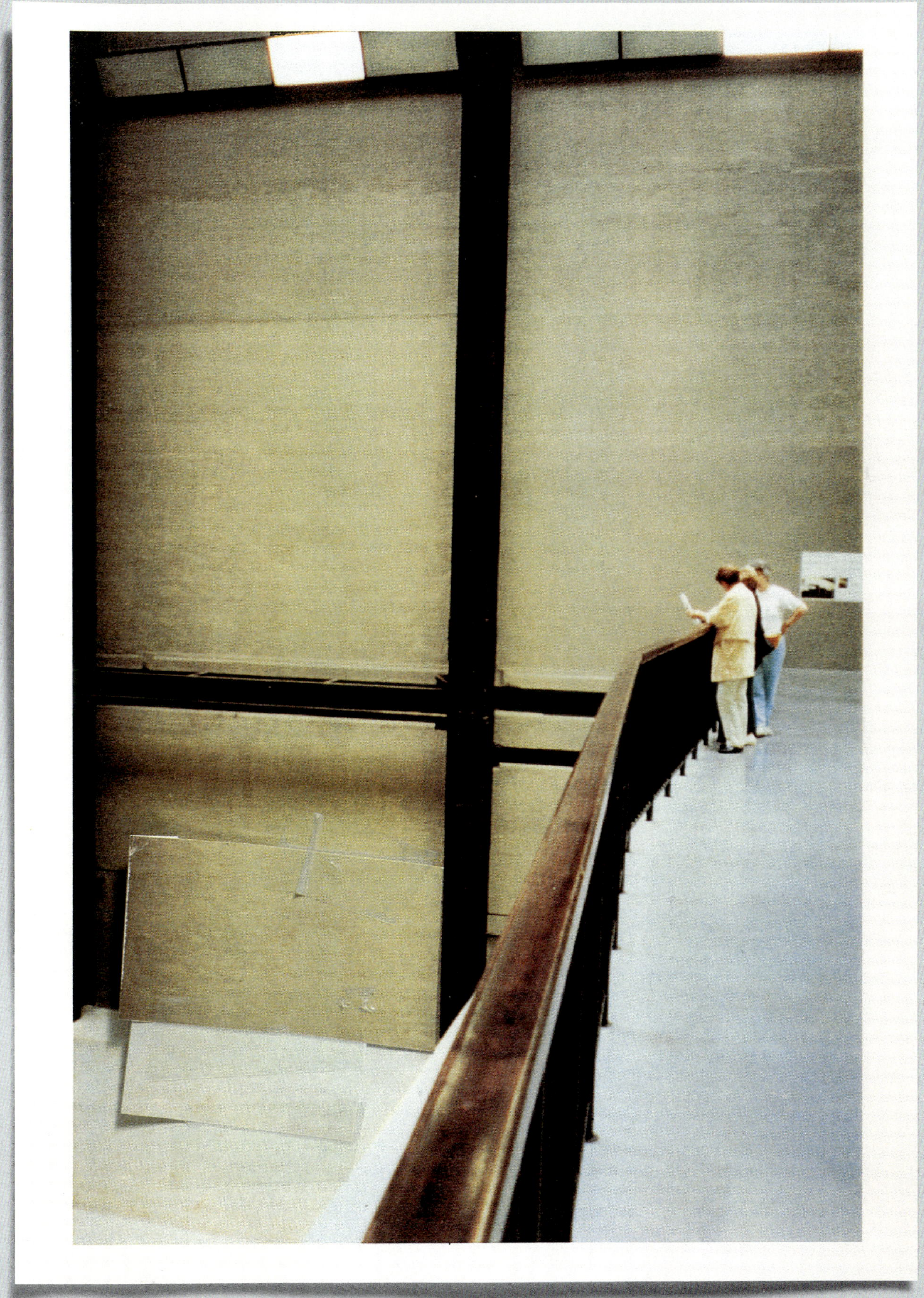

JUAN MUÑOZ
AV. PEÑALAR 20
TORRELODONES
MADRID 28250

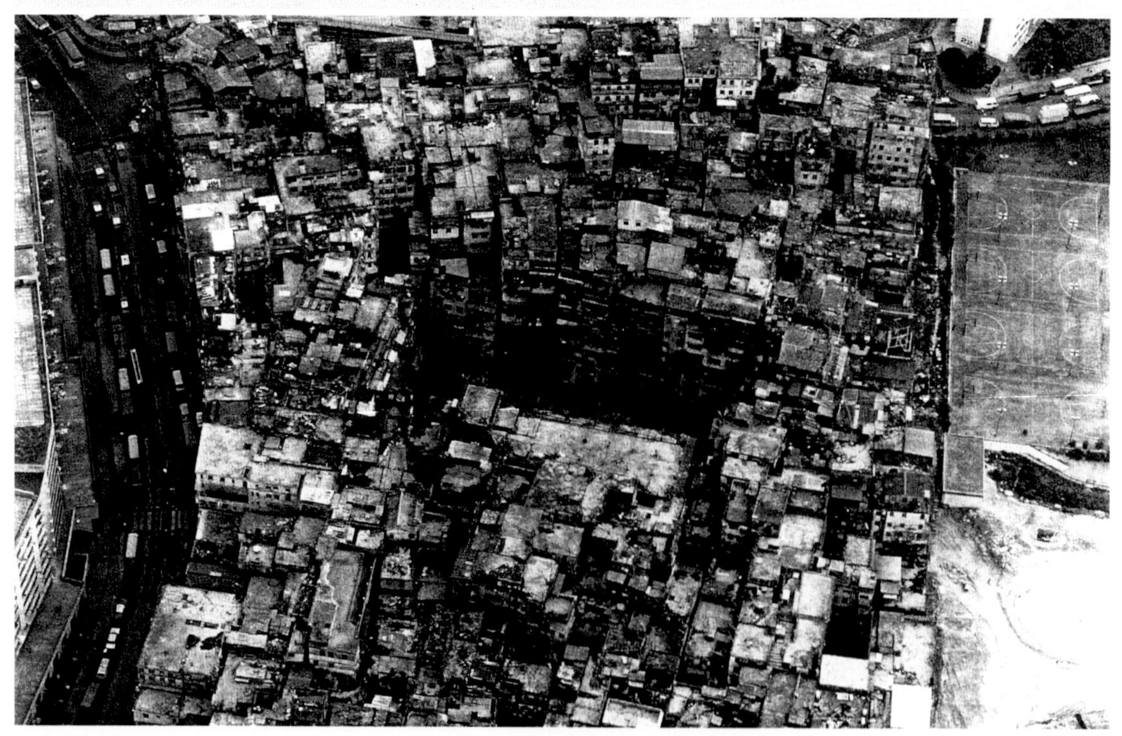

STONES AT REST

Geometry has to make itself stone before the word can make itself flesh… The object apprehended by Galileo required two worlds, or rather two spaces and one time. The incandescent space of geometry and the dark world of opaque mass. Nothing is so easy as to understand the first – it is there only to understand and be understood; nothing is so easy to hear as the word – it is there to be heard; but nothing so obscure as the second – nothing so difficult to conceive as the body, flesh or stone, nothing so hard to hear as the sound that escapes from it; nothing is so difficult as to know how it receives and envelops light.

MICHAEL SERRES, *Rome: The Book of Foundations*

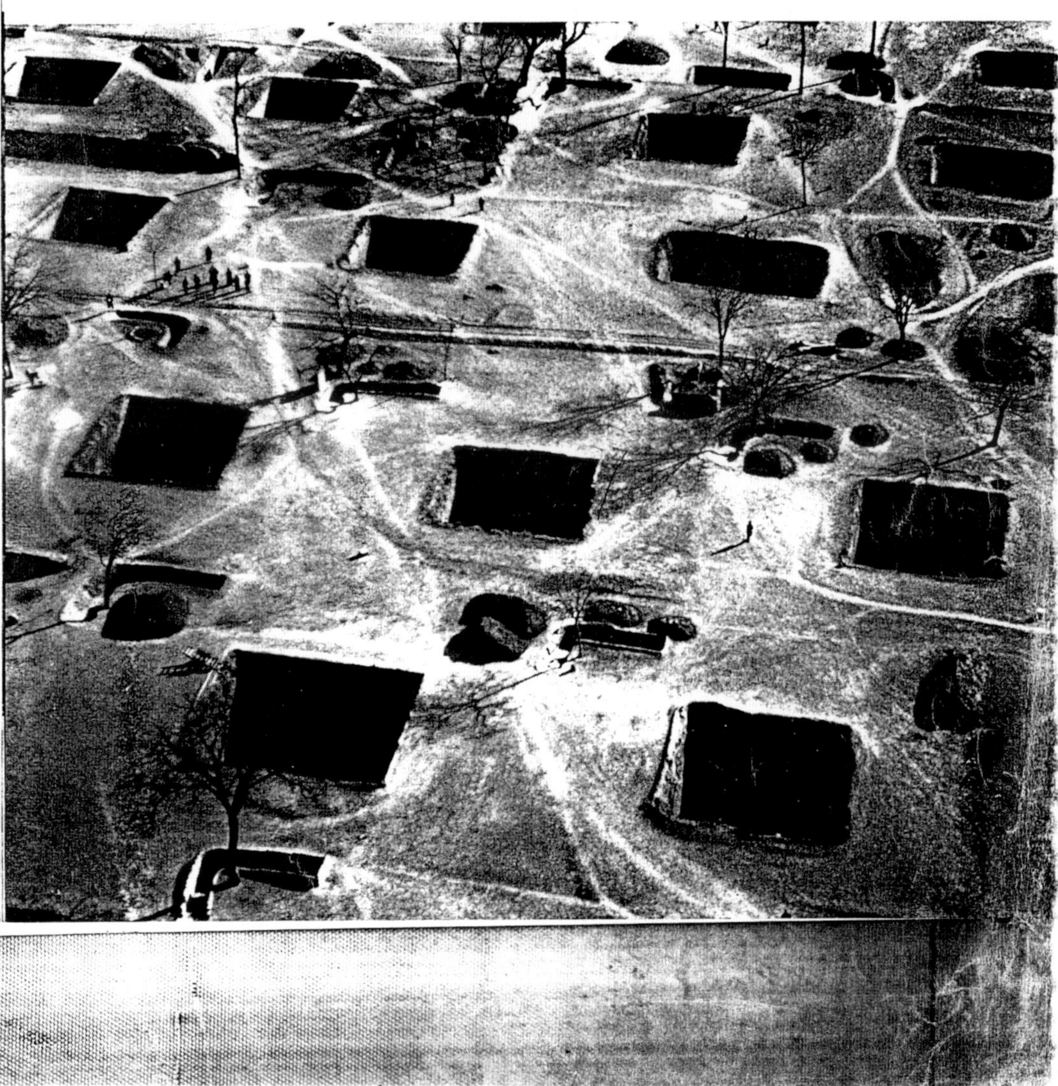

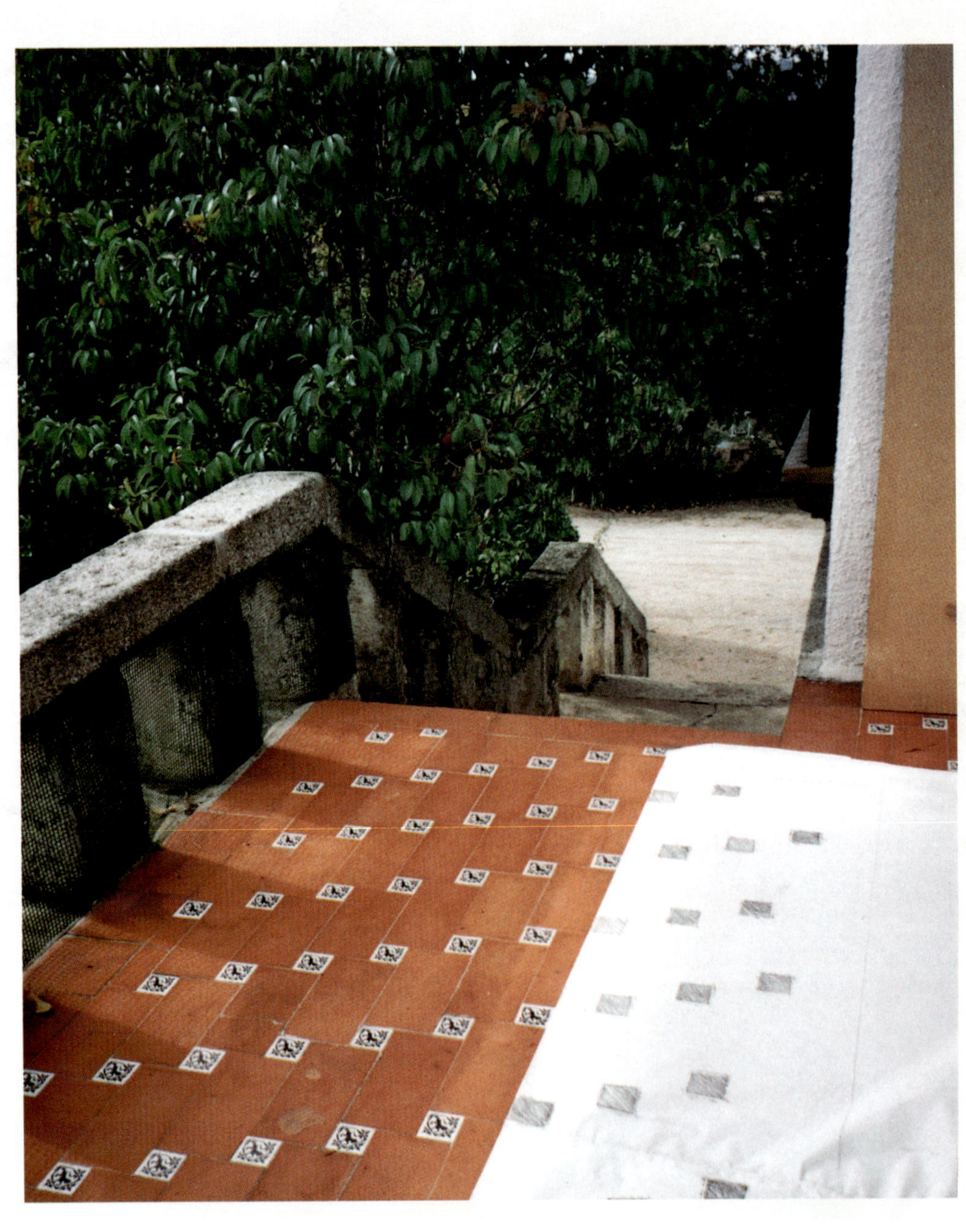

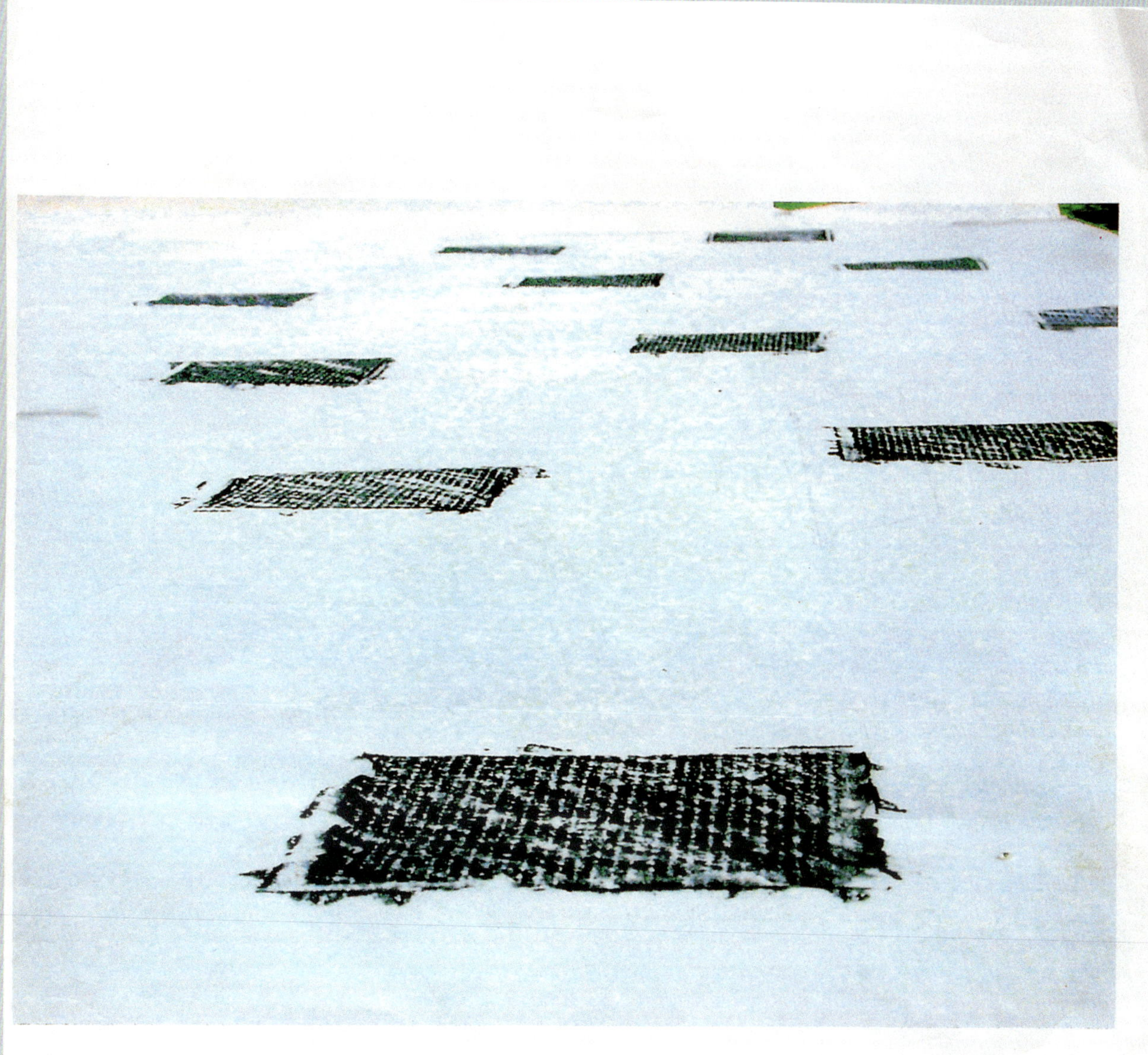

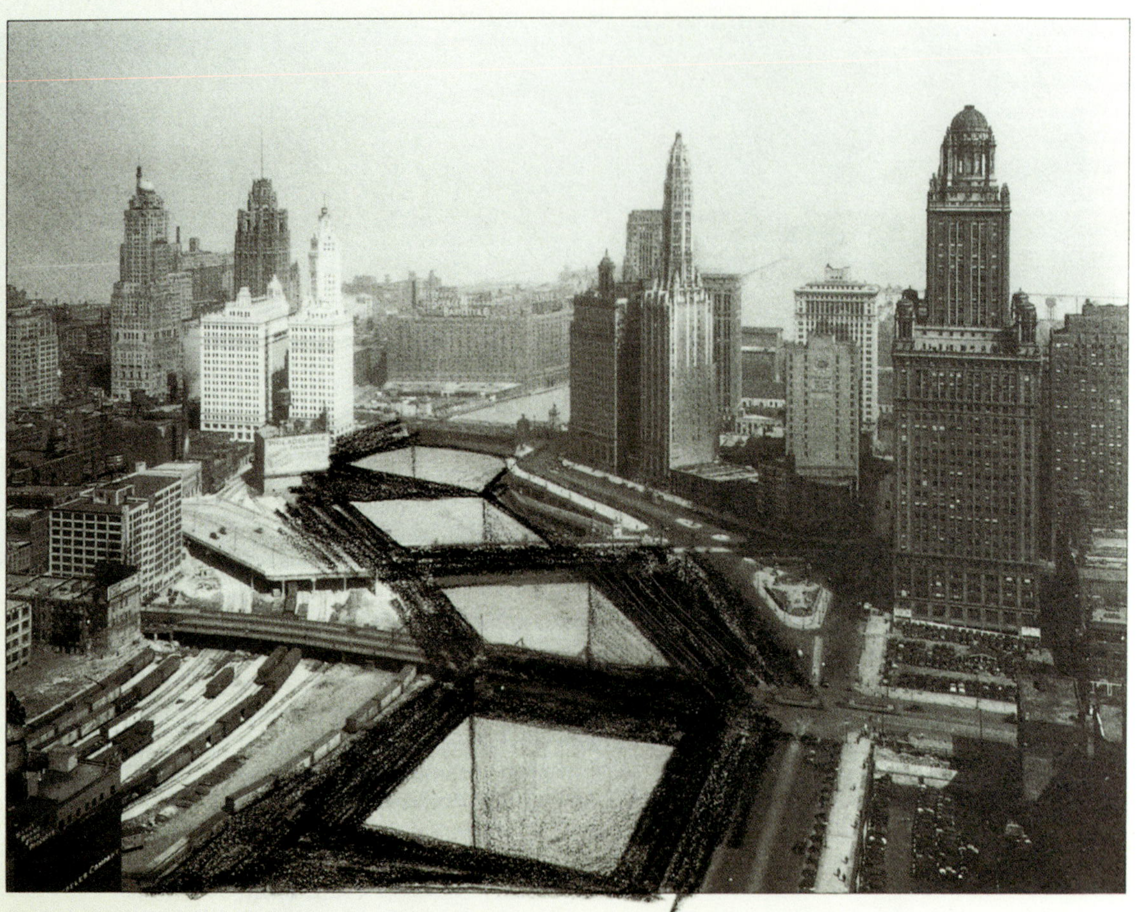

Figure 5. The Chicago River and Wacker Drive, aerial view eastward, 1931.

streets, including some that later connected with Wacker Drive. Federal regulations required a clear span of 140 feet, and to this day federal law requires that bascule bridges in the center of Chicago be kept in working order, even though commercial shipping long ago deserted this river.

By 1925, when construction began on Wacker Drive, the river's Main Branch was finally able to accommodate the passage, if not the docking and unloading, of large lake freighters. But the volume of shipping had continued to decline as other ports developed superior facilities, as rail transportation became cheaper, and as lumbering operations moved away from the shores of Lake Michigan.[15] From the successful lobbying of Congress by river interests had come navigational improvements all along the river, but not in time to make the construction of publicly financed commercial docks anywhere on its length a feasible proposition. So when the downtown riverfront was finally reconstructed, it was

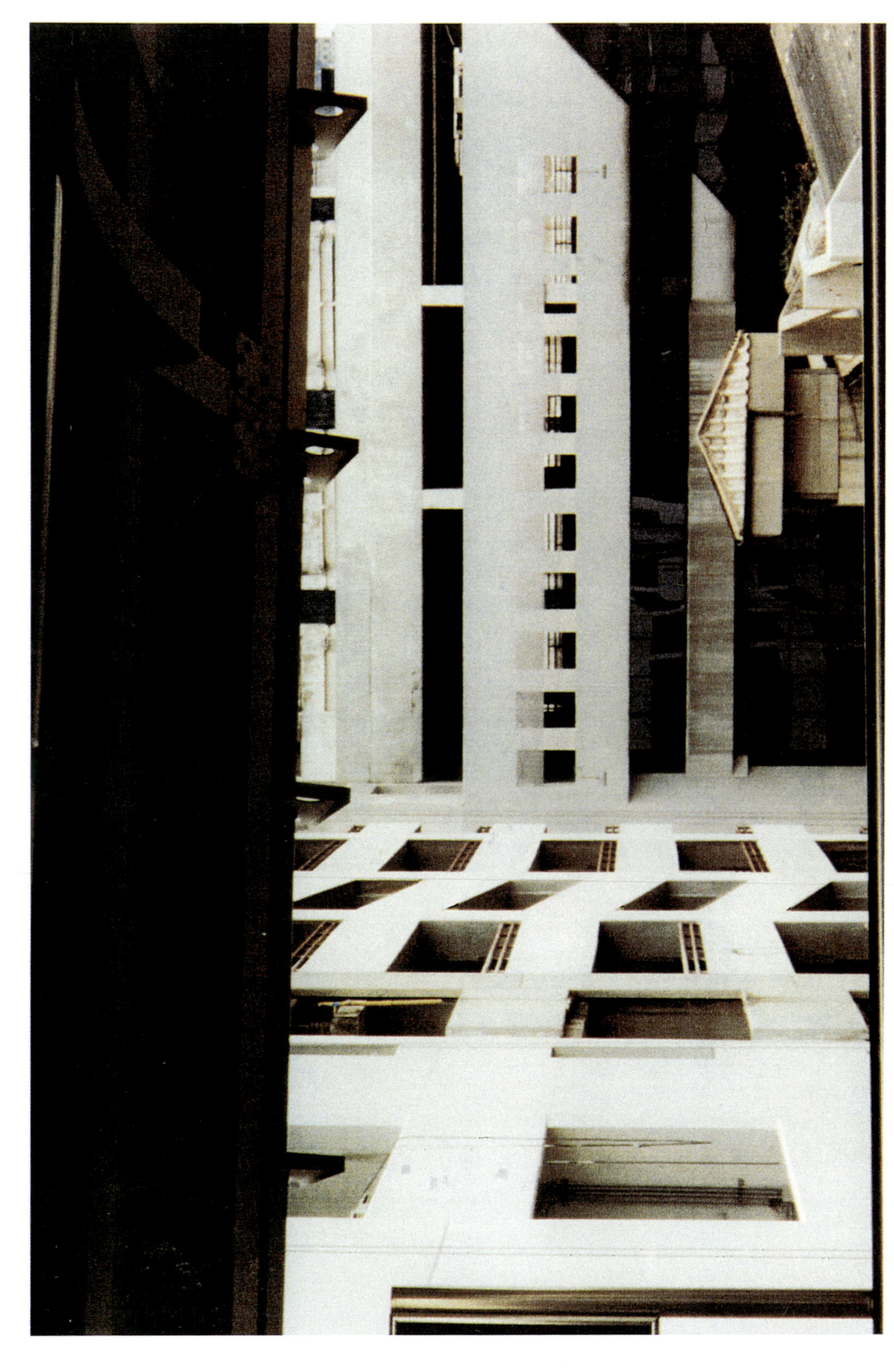

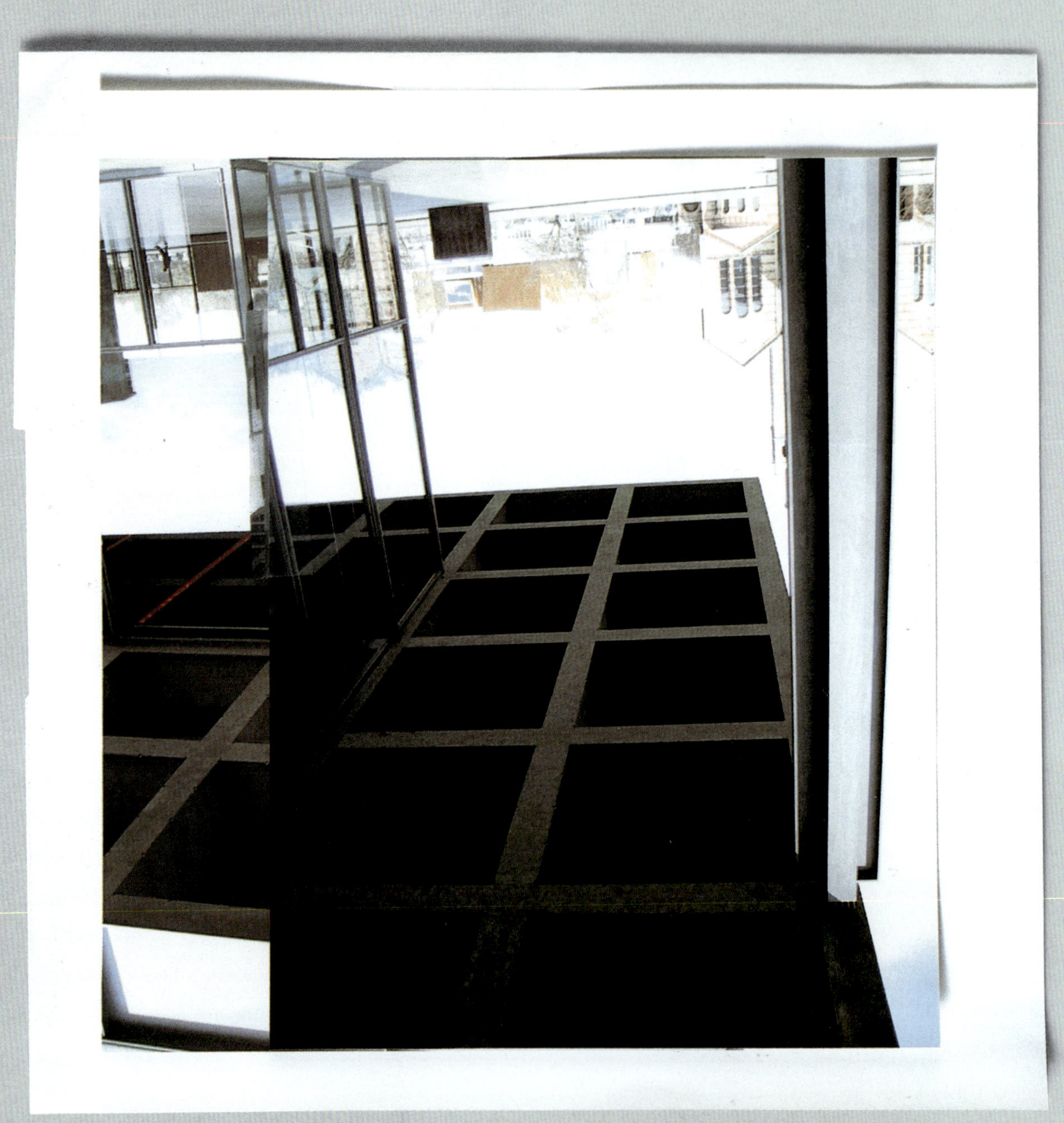

Witte de With

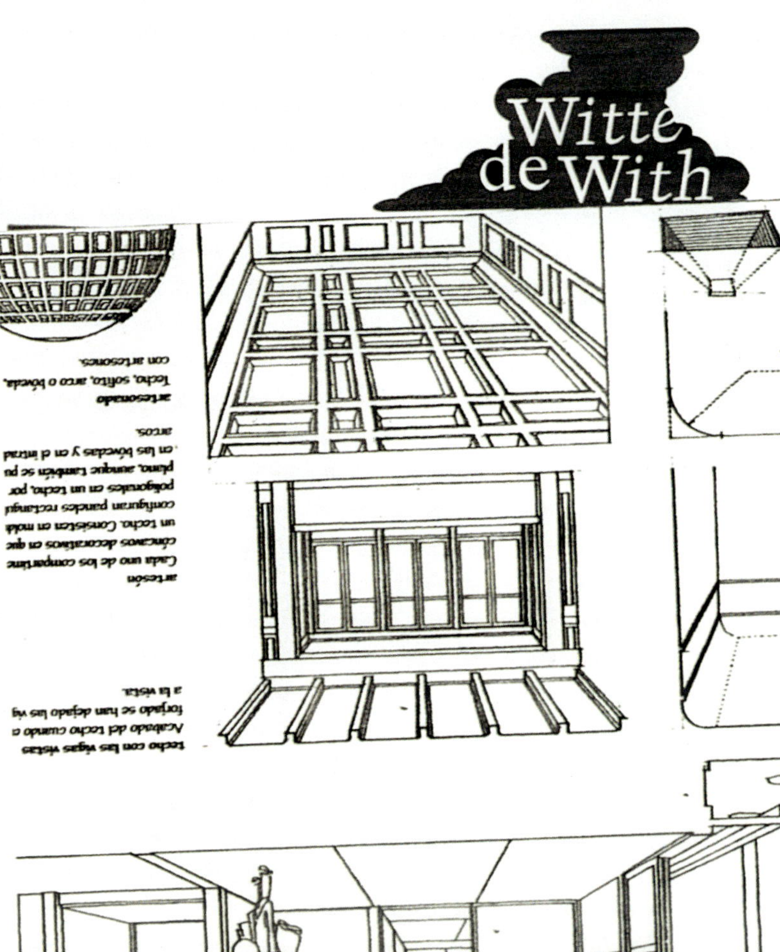

techo con las vigas vistas
Acabado del techo cuando al forjado se han dejado las vig[as] a la vista.

artesón
Cada uno de los compartime[ntos] cóncavos decorativos en que [se divide] un techo. Consisten en mold[uras que] configuran paneles rectangu[lares o] poligonales en un techo, por [lo general] plana, aunque también se pu[eden usar] en las bóvedas y en el intrad[ós de] arcos.

artesonado
Techo, sofito, arco o bóveda, con artesones.

puerta de mano izquierda, left-hand 150
puerta de mano izquierda de apertura hacia el
  exterior, left-hand reverse 150
puerta de paneles, paneled door 242
puerta de piso, hoistway door 26
puerta de salida de planta, exit door 239
puerta de salida de planta a otro sector,
  horizontal exit 239
puerta de tablas enlistonada, batten door 242
puerta de tableros, paneled door 242
puerta de vaivén, double-acting door 240
puerta de vidrio, glass door 242
puerta doble, double doors 240
puerta forrada de metal calaminado, kalamein
  door 243
puerta galilea, galilee porch 175
puerta giratoria, revolving door 240
puerta giratoria de simple efecto, single-acting
  door 240
puerta holandesa, Dutch door 242
puerta levadiza, overhead door 240
puerta lisa, flush door 243
puerta maciza, solid-core door 243
puerta metálica de alma hueca, hollow-metal door
  243
puerta monumental, portal 98
puerta oculta, gib door, jib door 242
puerta plegable, folding door 240
puerta plegable doble de dos hojas, bifold door
  240
puerta precolgada, prehung door 243
puerta resistente al fuego, fire door 237
puerta veneciana, Venetian door 241
puerta-pantalla, screen door 242
puerta, door 240-243
puerta abatible, swinging door 240
puerta antisonora, acoustical door, sound-
  insulating door 243
puerta arrollable, rolling door 240
puerta automática, automatic door 240
puerta basculante, pivoted door 240
puerta ciega, blind door 97
puerta cochera, carriage porch, porte-cochère 98
puerta combinable, combination door 242
puerta compensada, balanced door 240
puerta corredera, sliding door 240
puerta corredera con cámara, pocket door 240
puerta cristalera, casement door, French door
  242
puerta de acordeón, accordion door 240
puerta de alma hueca, hollow-core door 243
puerta de doble hoja, double doors 240
puerta de dos hojas, double doors 240
puerta de lamas, blind door, louvered door 242
puerta de mano derecha, right-hand 150

Te envío luego las imágenes.

Un abrazo

Witte
de With
center for contemporary art

Witte de Withstraat 50, 3012 BR Rotterdam, tel +31(0)10 - 411 01 44, fax +31(0)10 - 411 79 24, e-mail info@wdw.nl, website www.wdw.nl

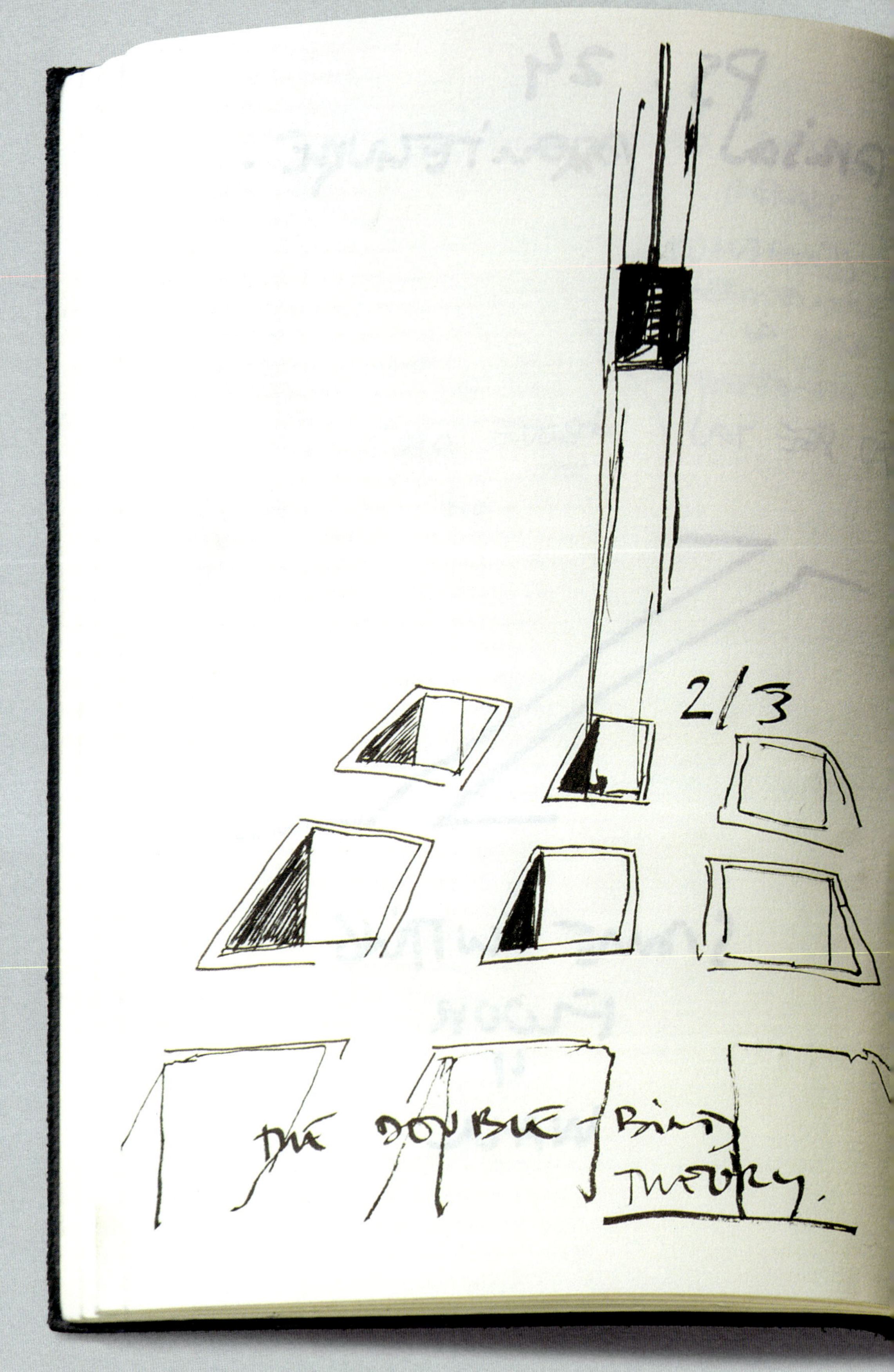

2/3
THE DOUBLE-BIND
THEORY.

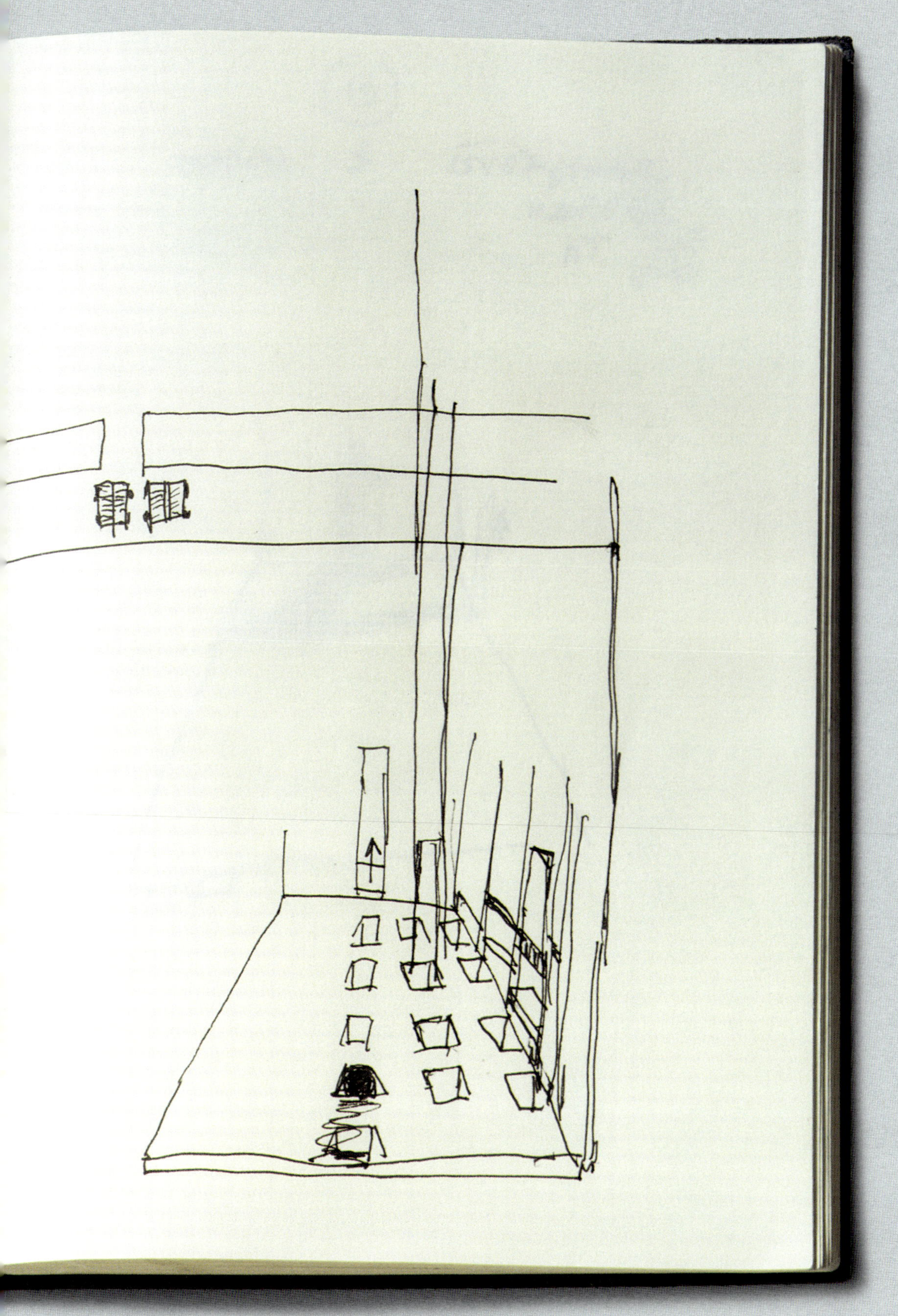

aveva solo cinque). Dove l'esempio brunelleschiano certo non soccorre è nella facciata, lasciata in sospeso da Filippo e discussa dai suoi continuatori. Il modello del Fugazza può essersi allontanato nettamente dal piano dell'88, considerando che la fabbrica era partita dal capocroce e forse la fronte era ancora da precisare. Il modello postbramantesco tiene conto di esempi come Santa Maria Novella a Firenze e Sant'Agostino a Roma, ma il marcapiano affidato a una galleria di arcate denuncia esempi lombardi, come il protiro, che ricompare in Santa Maria Nascente ad Abbiategrasso e nel piano UA 1 per San Pietro.

Più ci si allontana dall'impianto impostato nell'88 e più sono opinabili le indicazioni desumibili dal modello, anche per la difficoltà di distinguere gli elementi autenticamente bramanteschi da quelli filtrati nel linguaggio "riformato" dell'Amadeo e del Dolcebuono. La fabbrica pavese è senza dubbio un cantiere ambizioso, dalle estenuanti vicende costruttive, ma è indubbio che l'intervento bramantesco vi abbia impresso un significativo salto di qualità. È però leggibile solo in filigrana per la difficoltà di valutare quanto, del suo

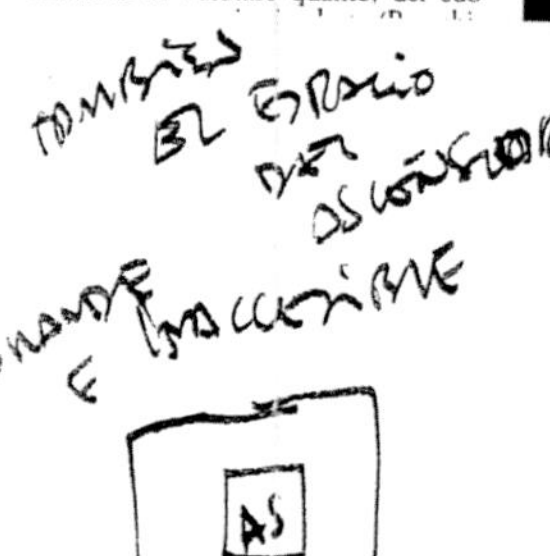

marcamente, nonostante comuni interessi dell'esecuzione e la presenza, in entrambi i cantieri, dell'Amadeo. Per Bramante un'occasione importante di ricerca, ma anche un ruolo complesso, defilato, non senza contrasti.

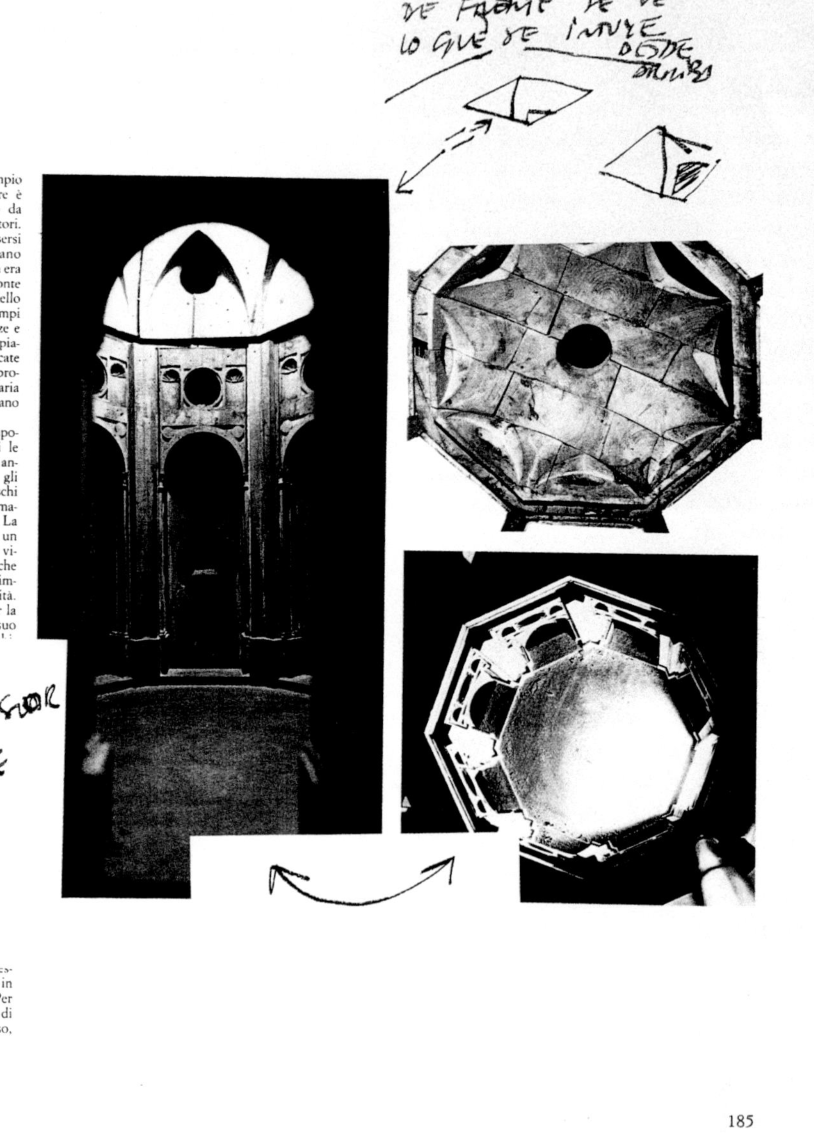

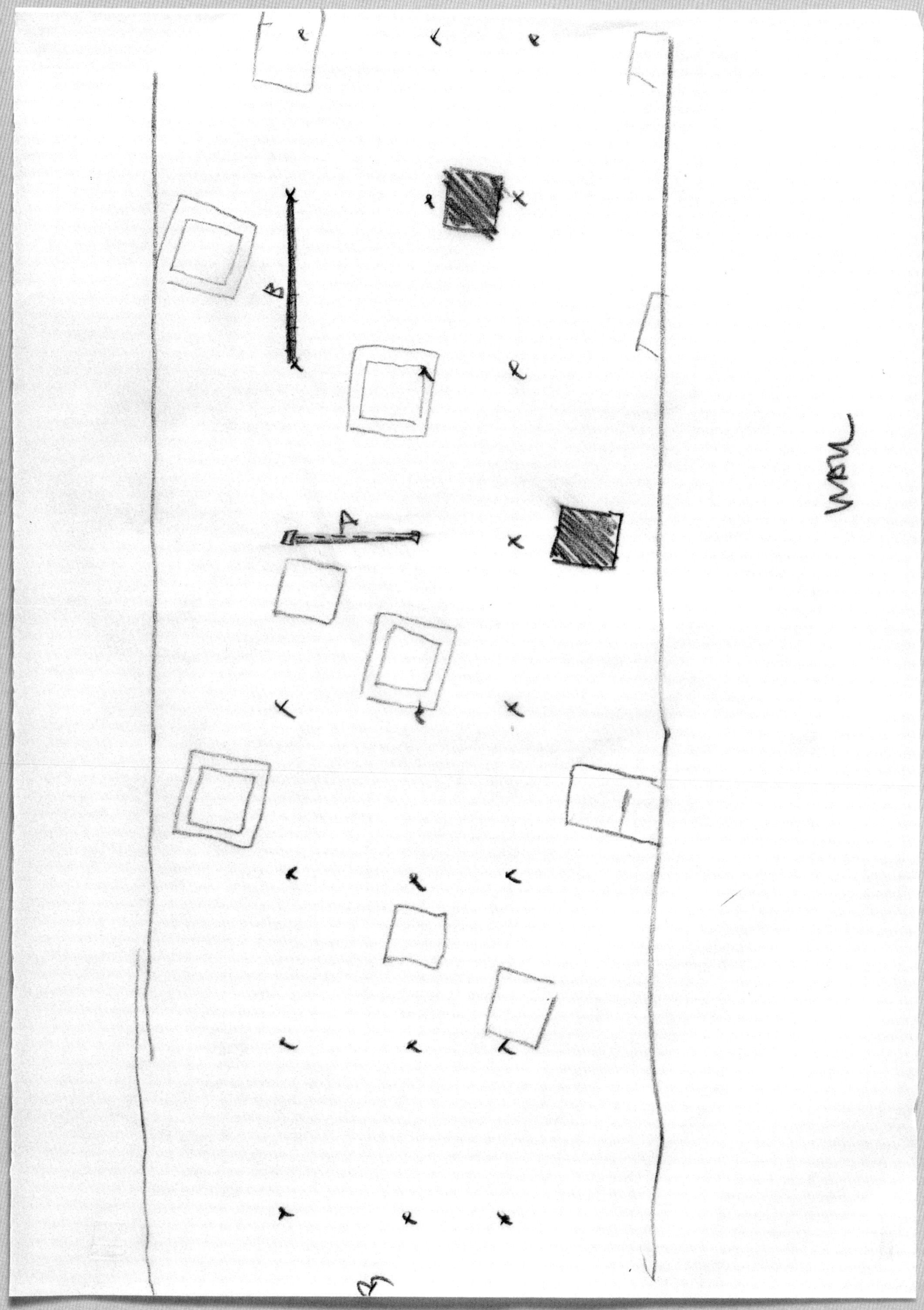

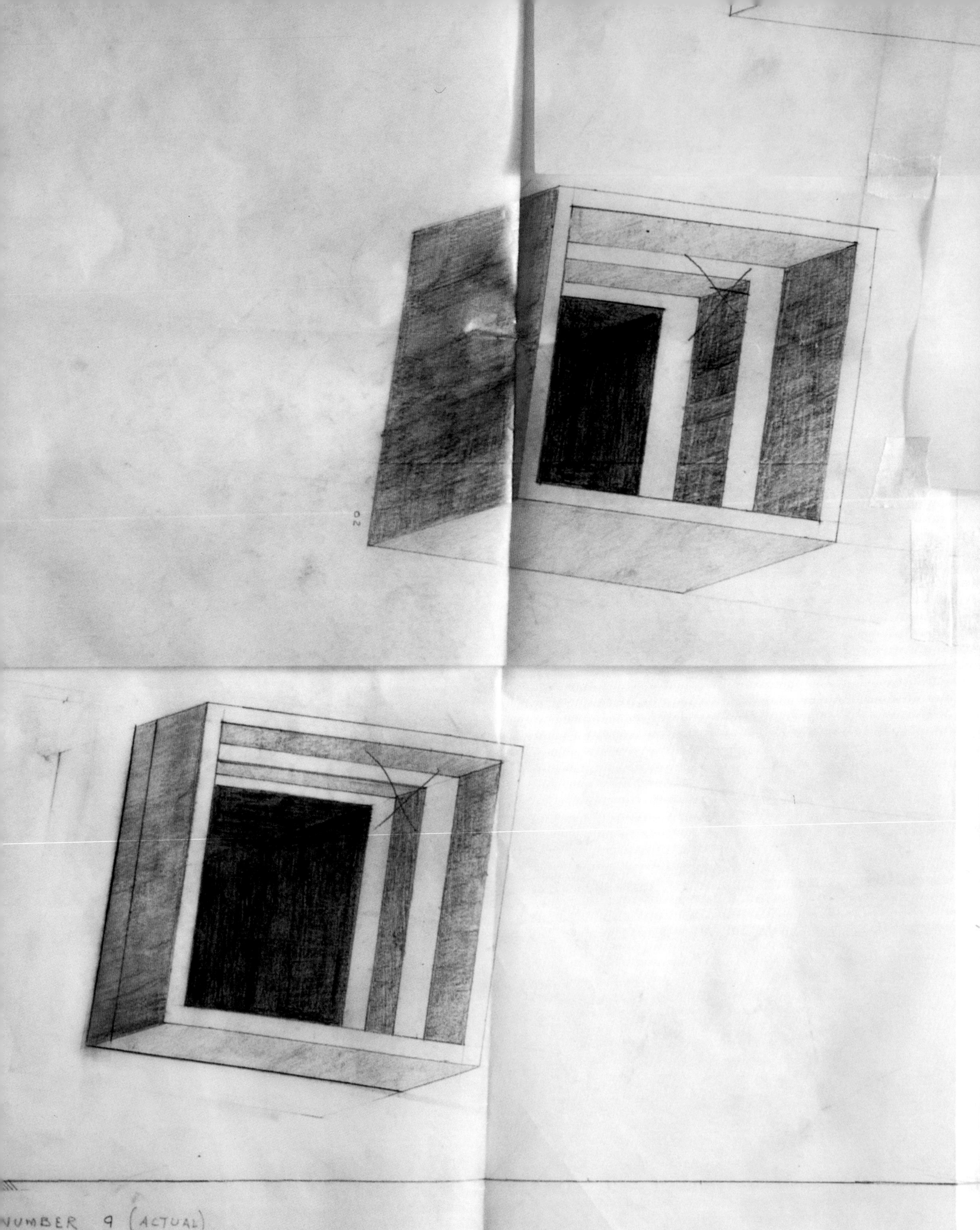
NUMBER 9 (ACTUAL).
17.50 (57'-0")

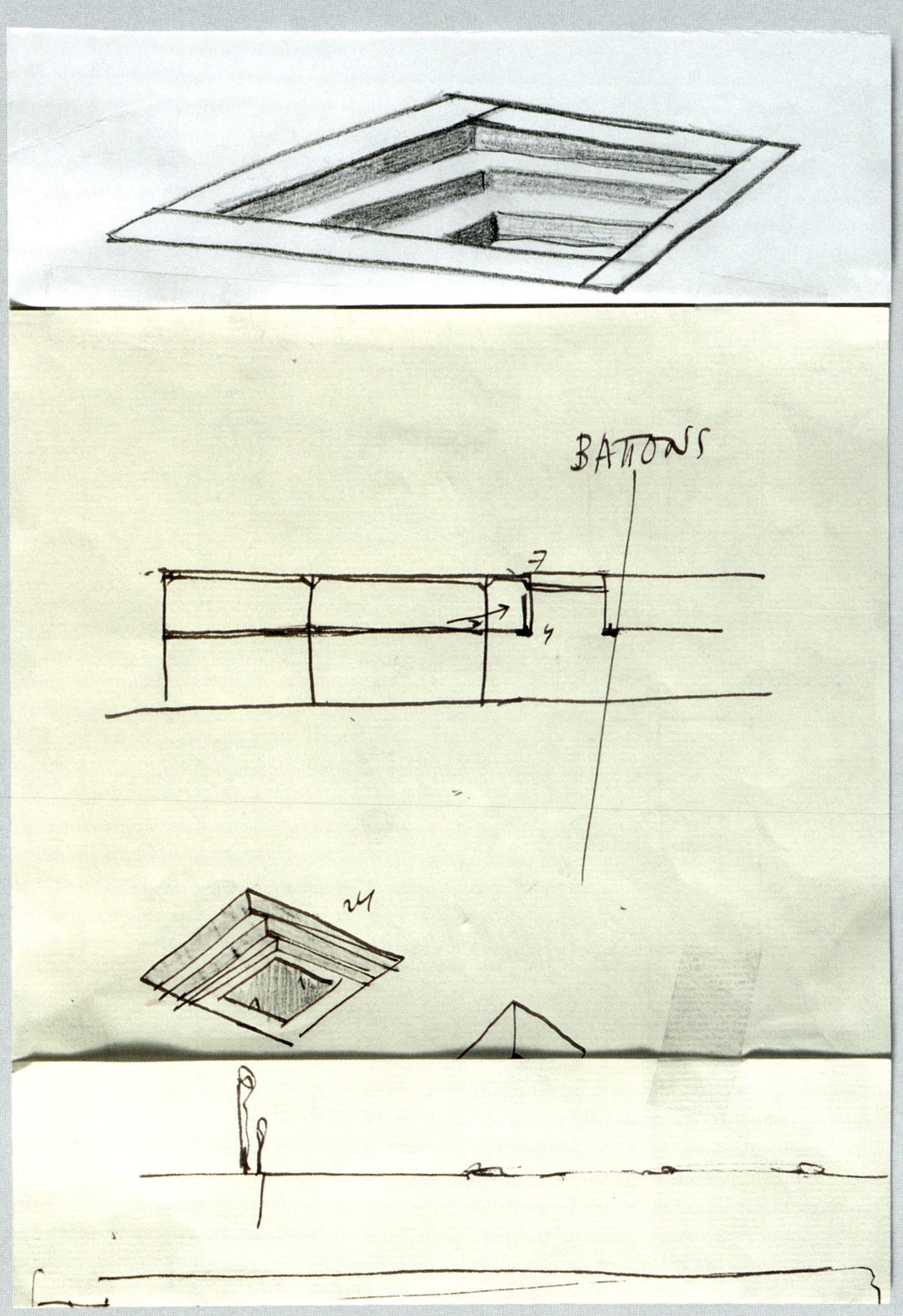

BATTONS

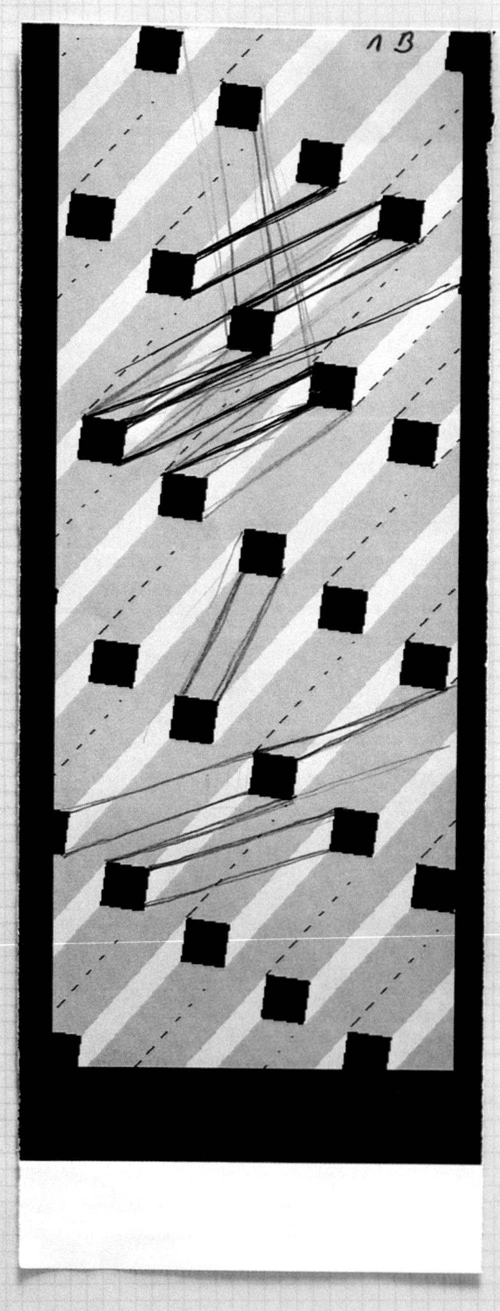
A B

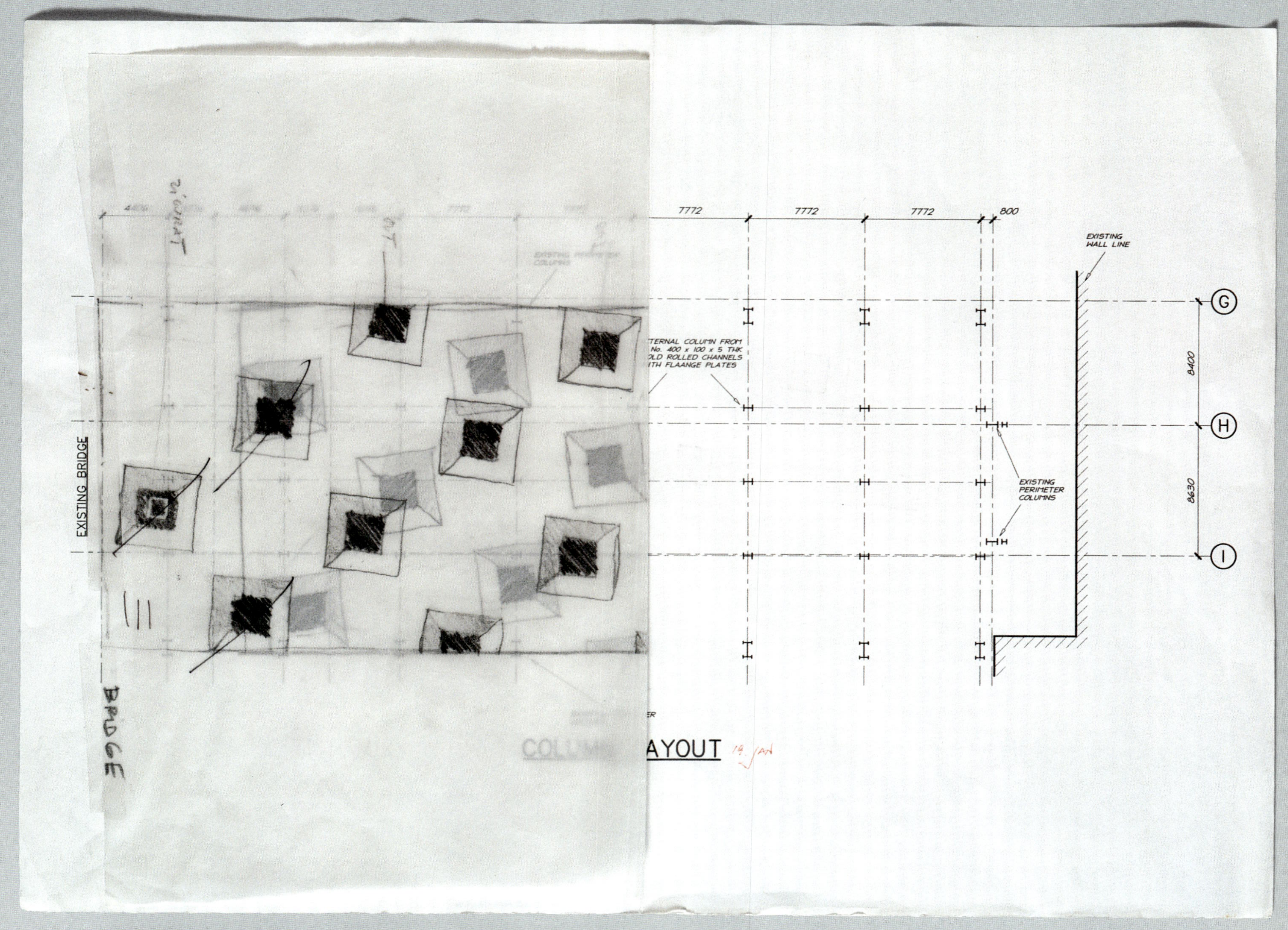

EXISTING BRIDGE
BRIDGE
COLUMN LAYOUT
EXISTING PERIMETER COLUMNS
INTERNAL COLUMN FROM
No. 400 x 100 x 5 THK
OLD ROLLED CHANNELS
WITH FLAANGE PLATES
EXISTING PERIMETER COLUMNS
EXISTING WALL LINE
7772
7772
7772
800
8400
8630
G
H
I

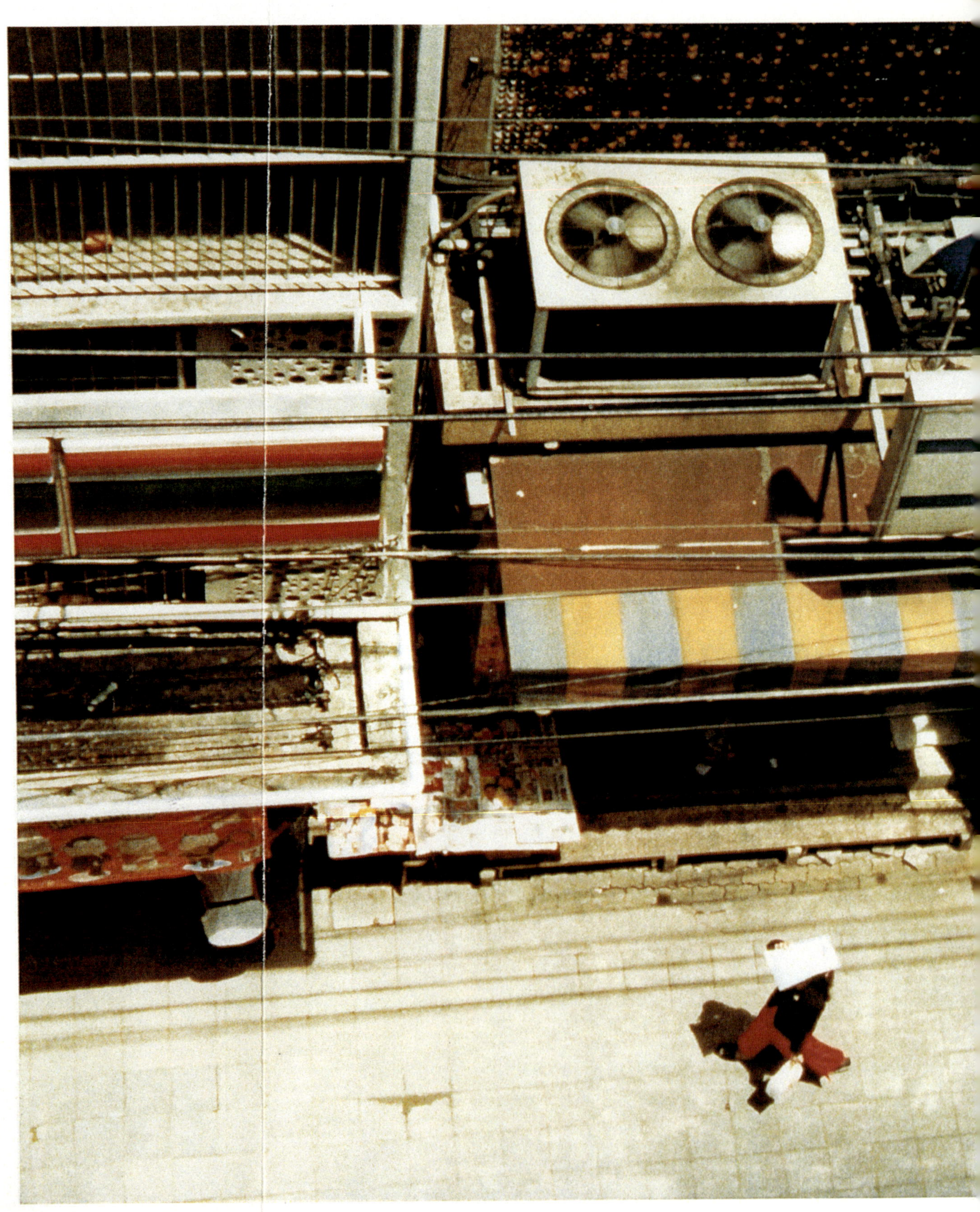

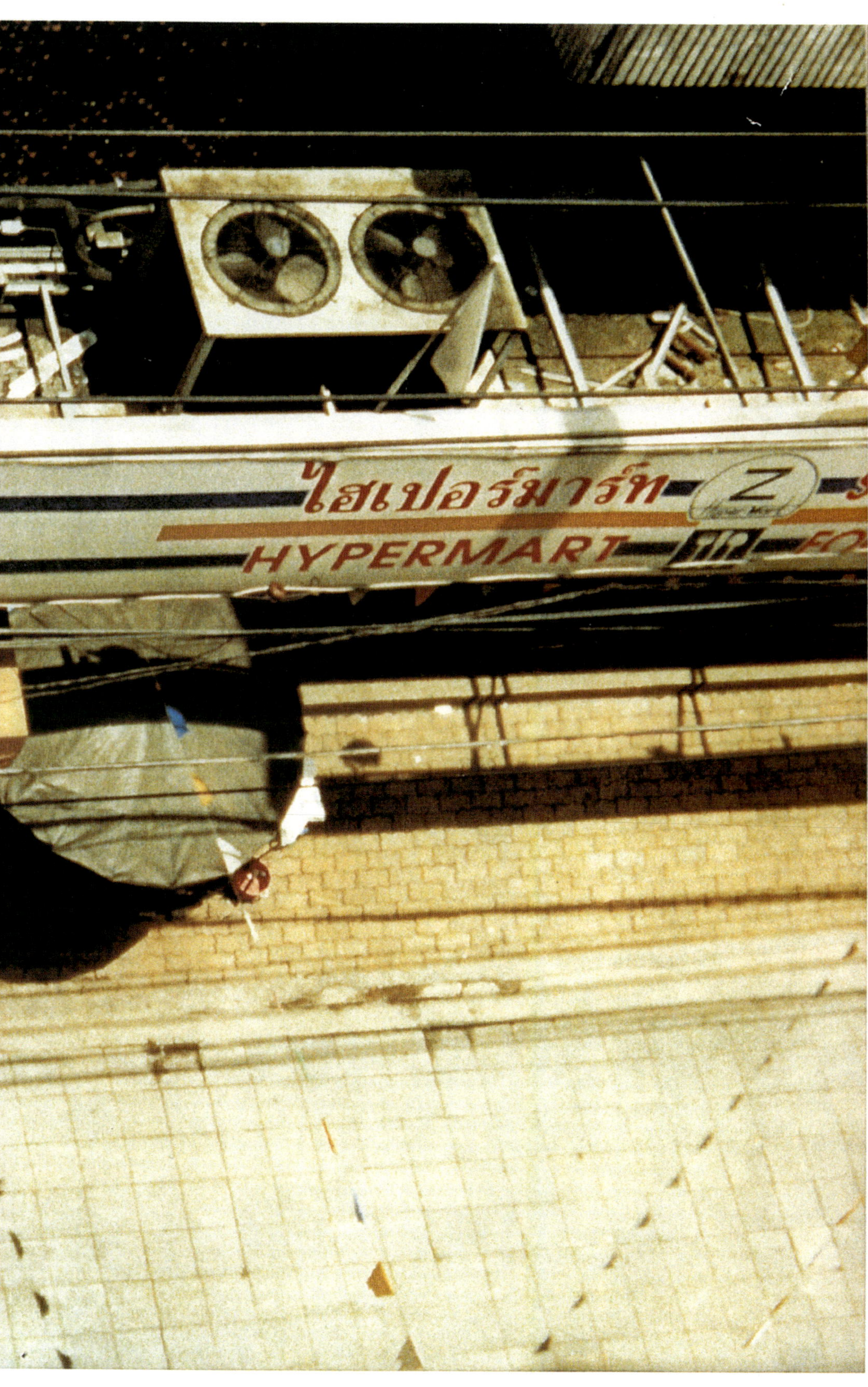

ไฮเปอร์มาร์ท
HYPERMART

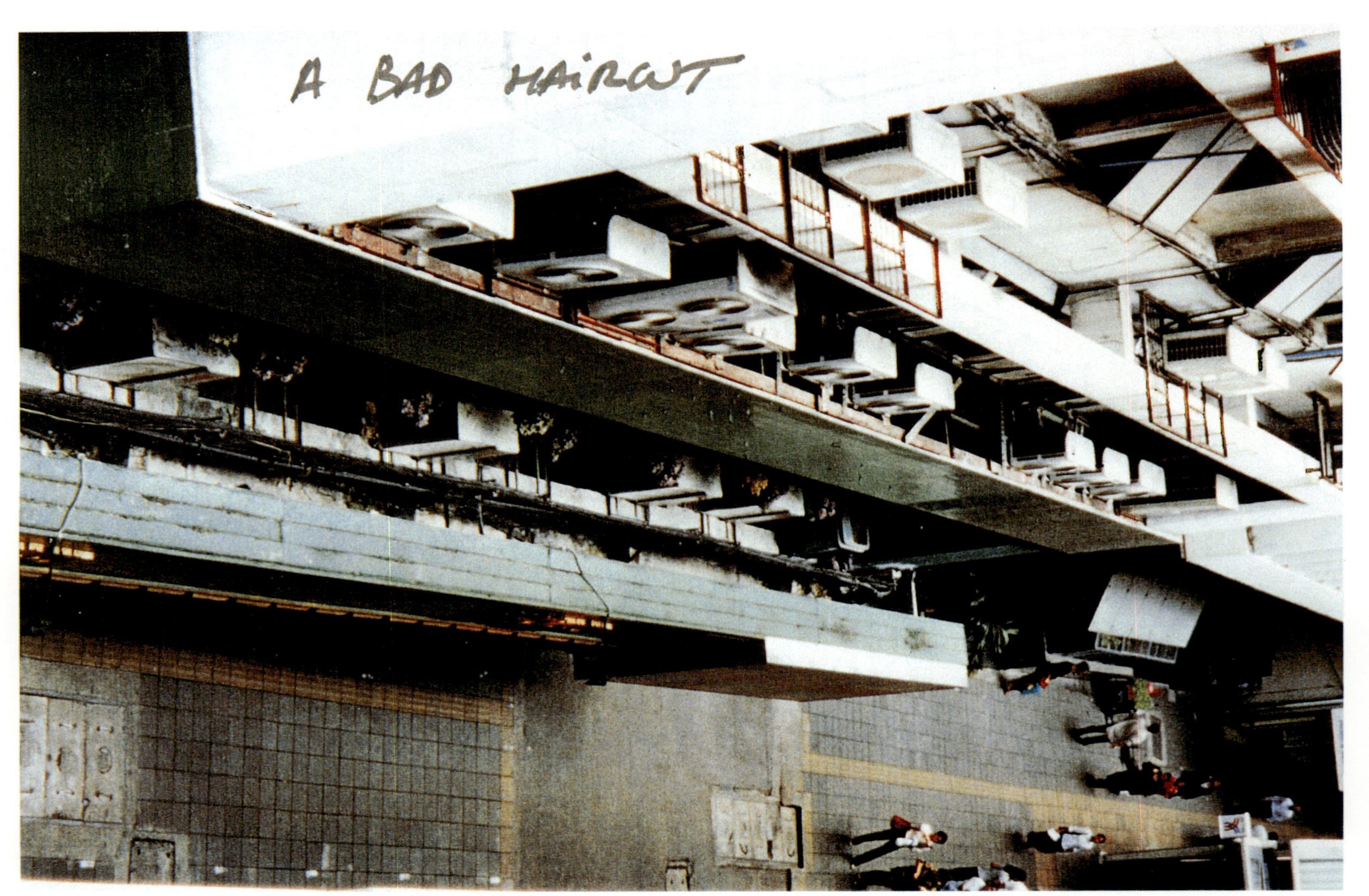

A BAD HAIRCUT

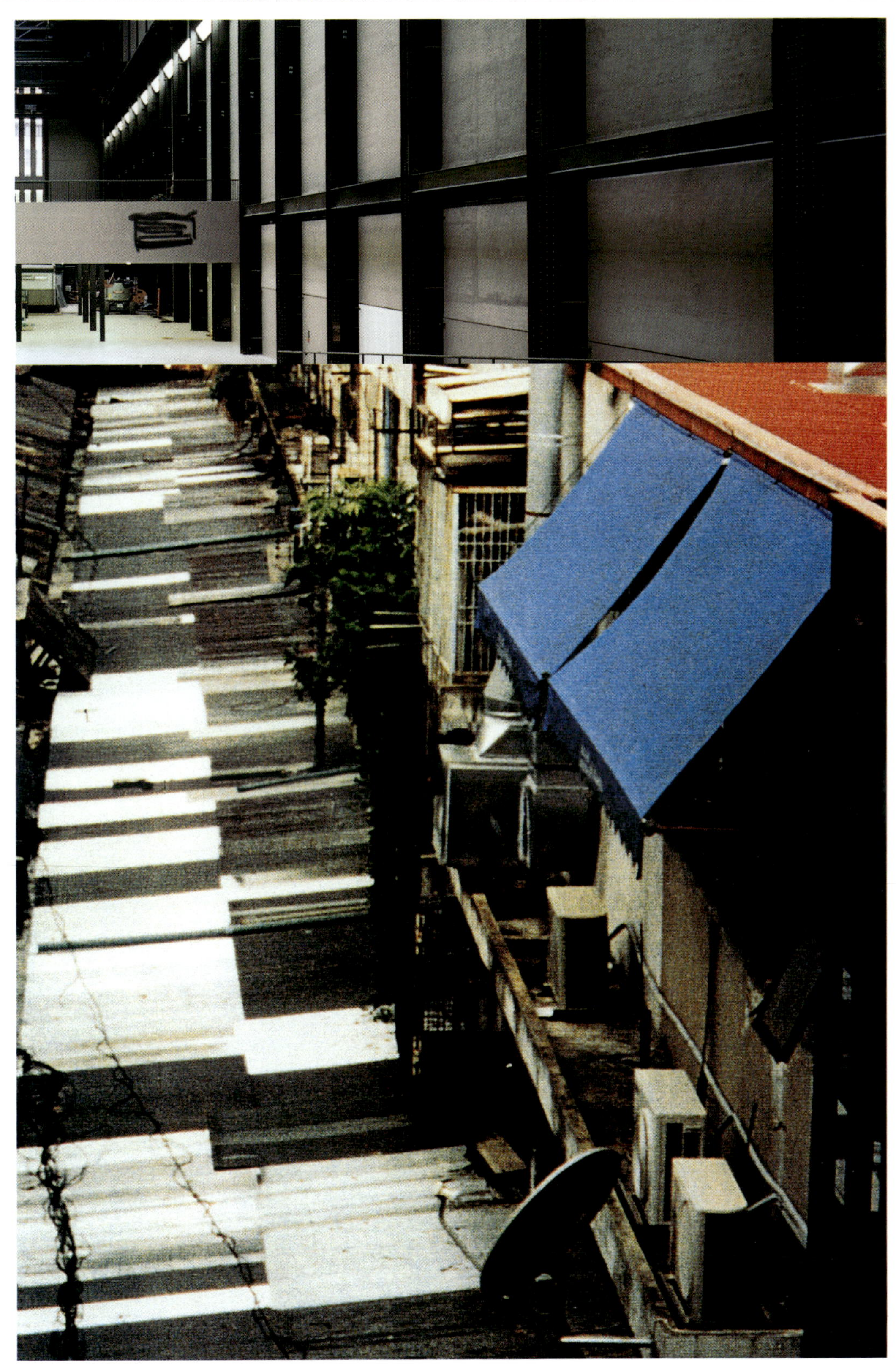

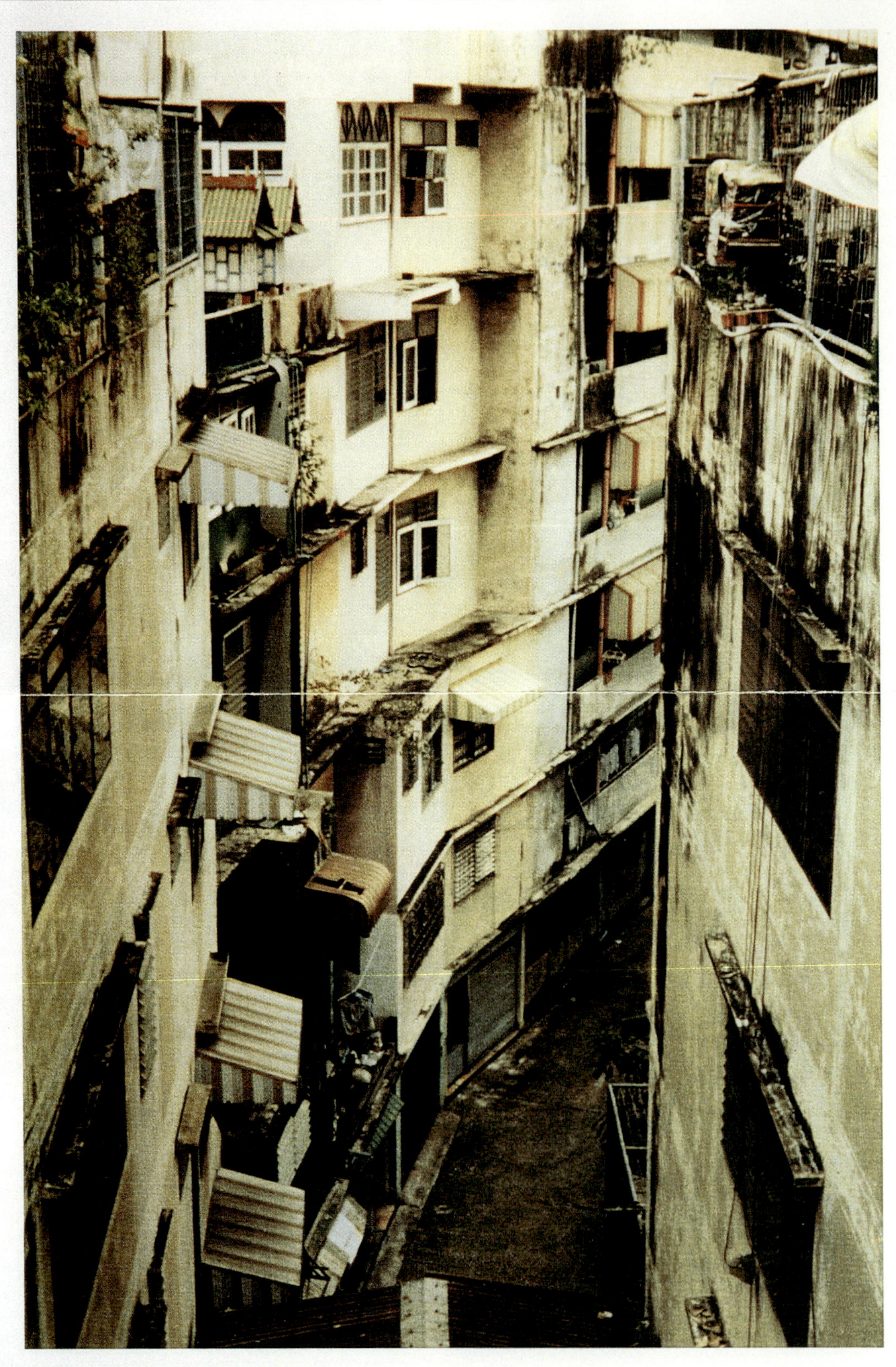

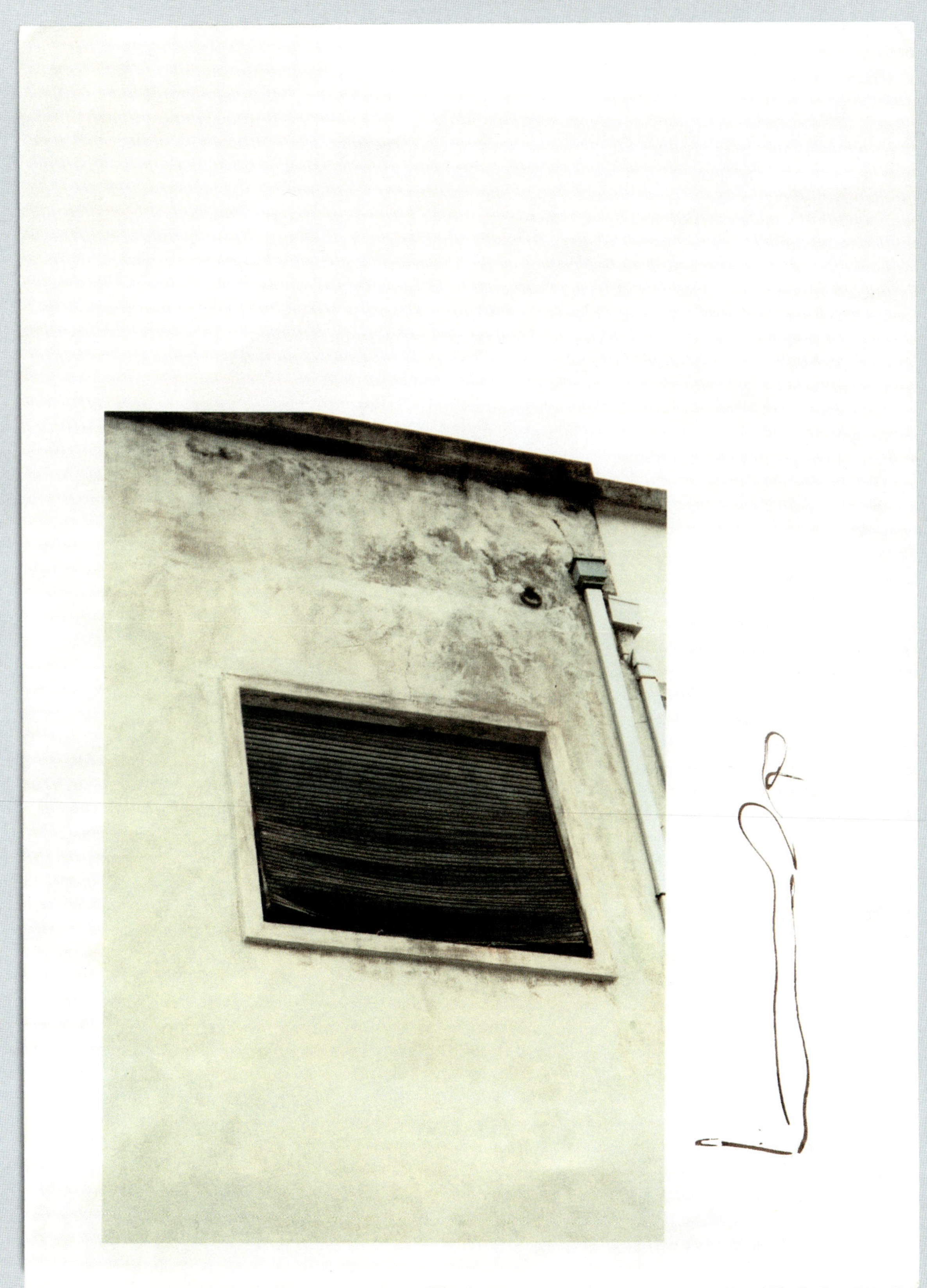

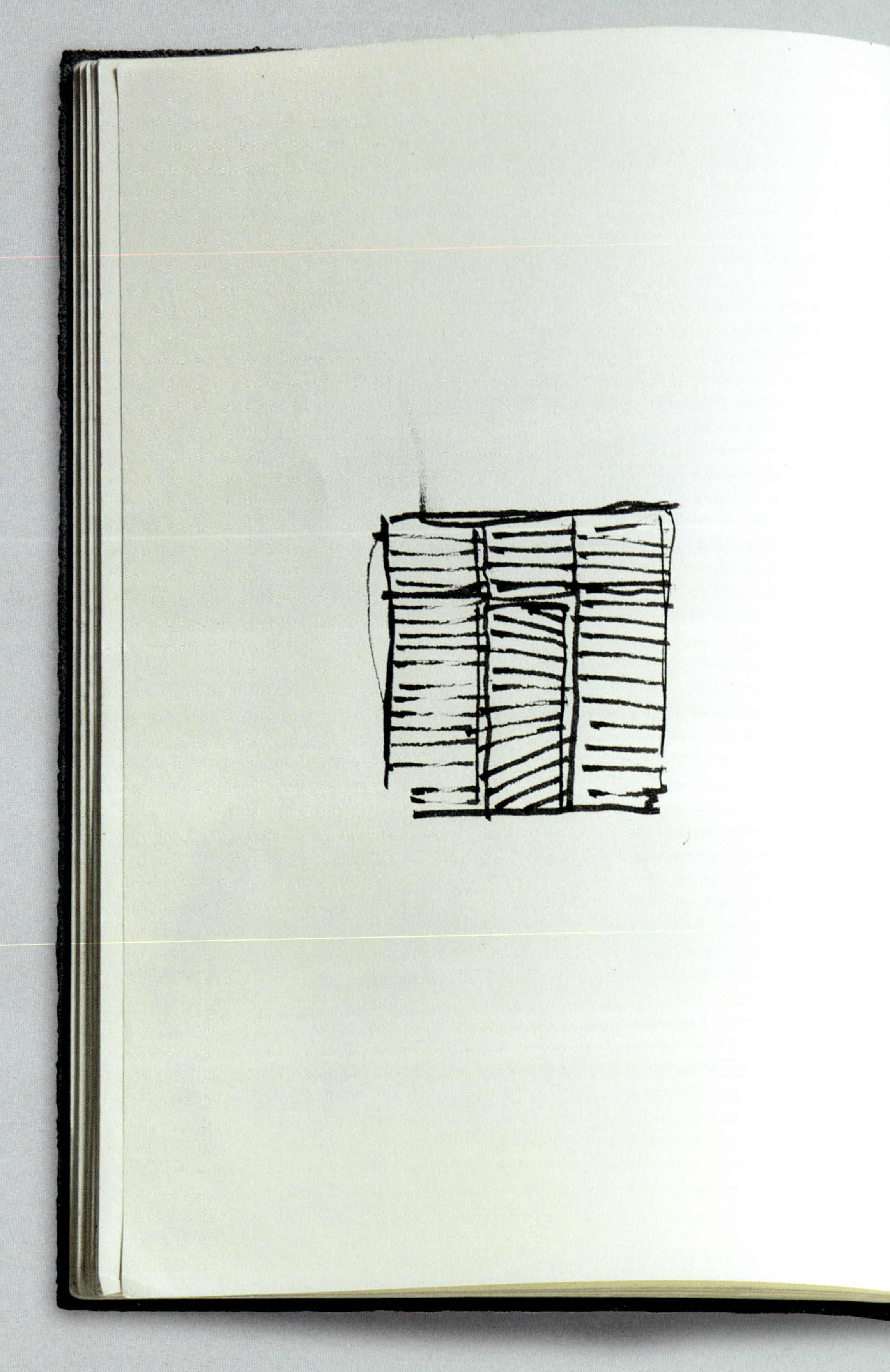

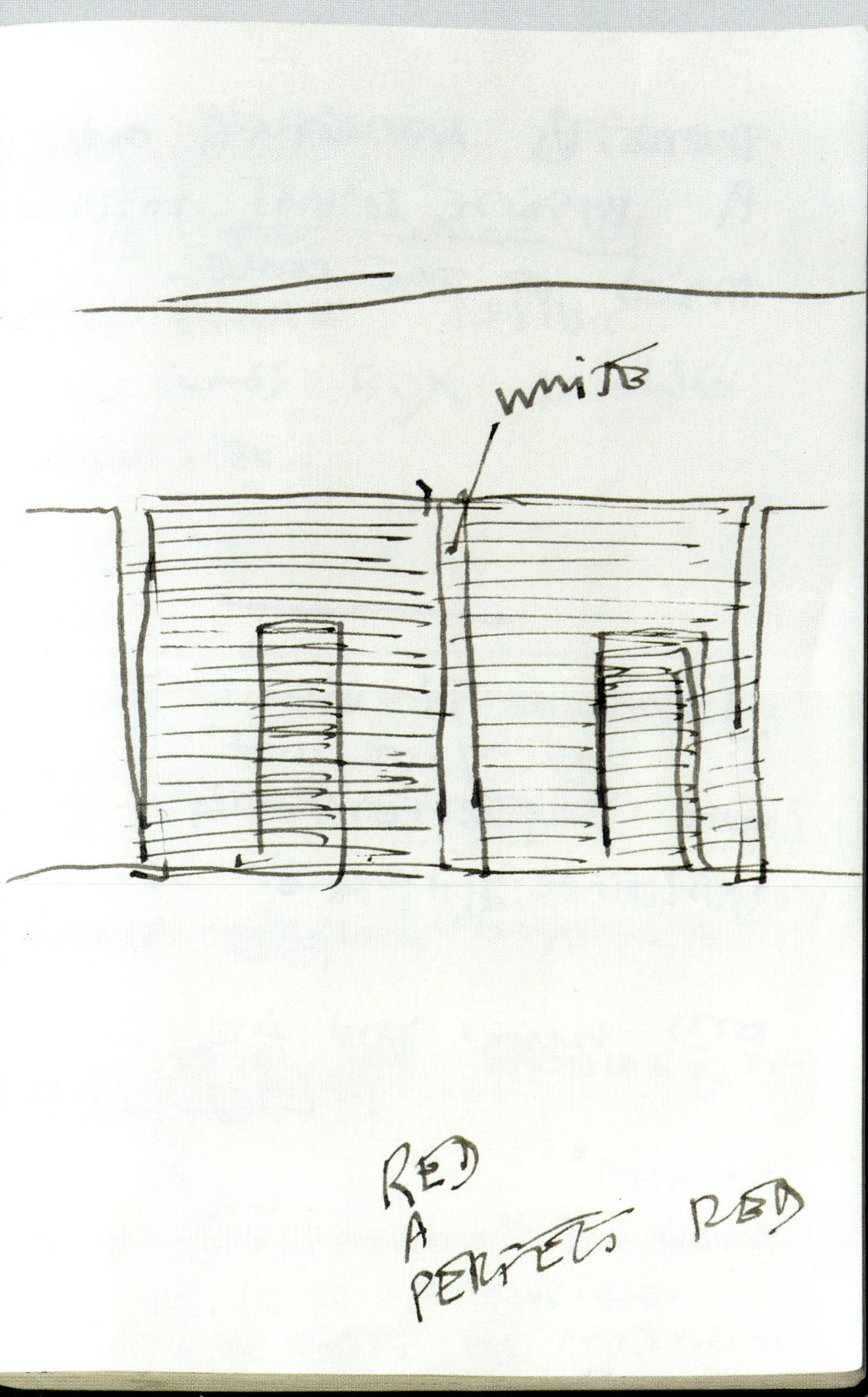

RED
A
PERFECT RED

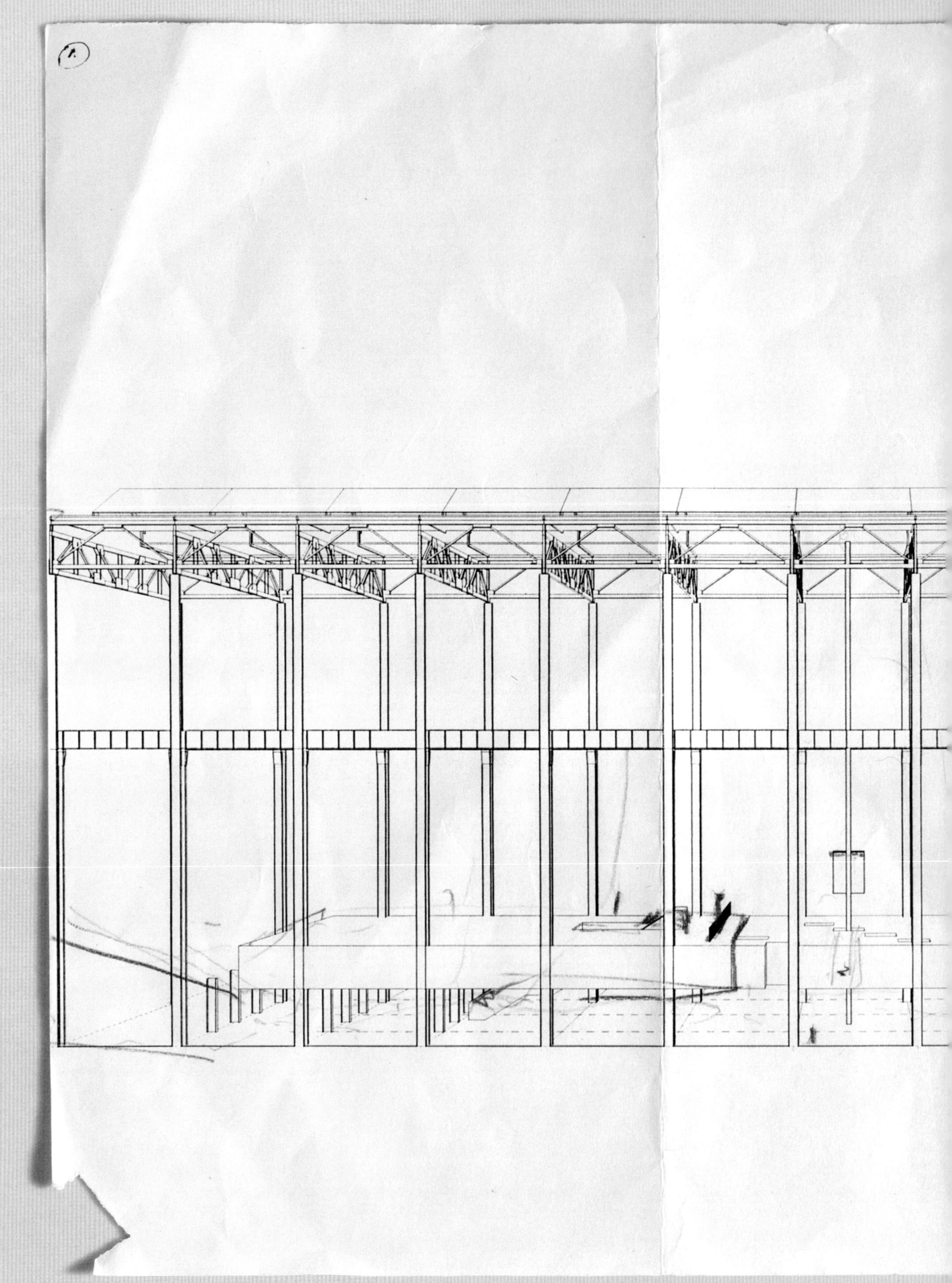

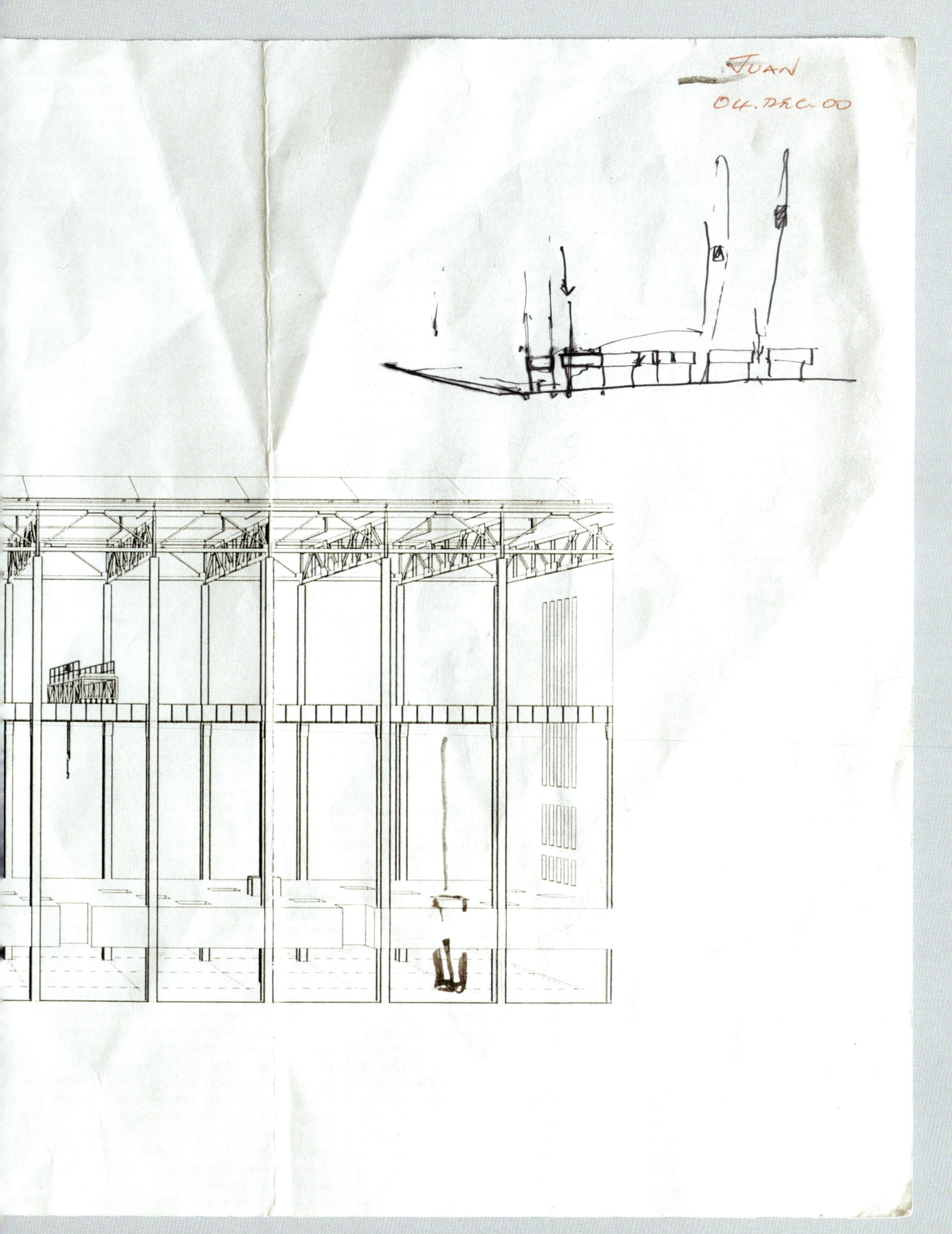

Juan
04. DEC. 00

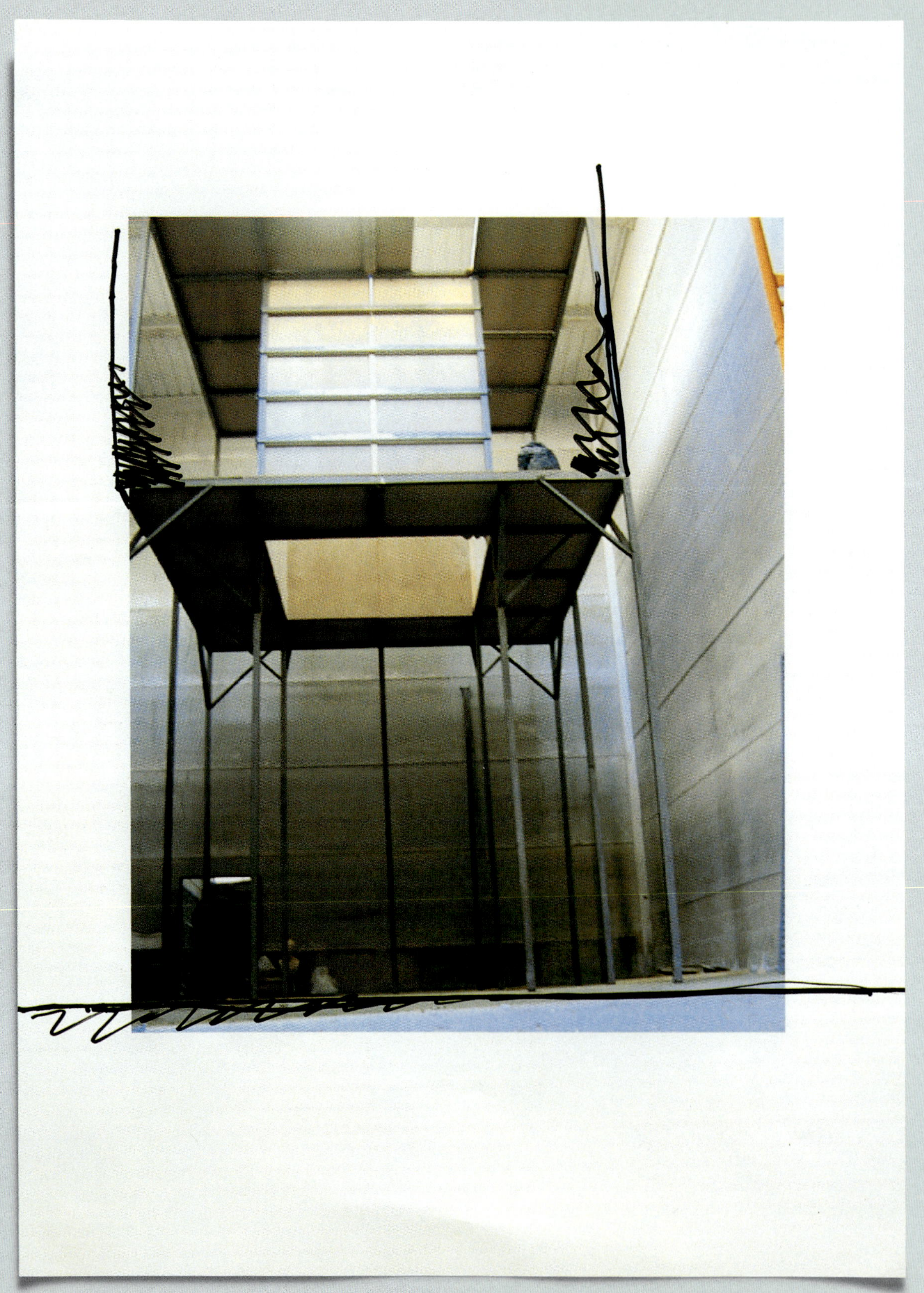

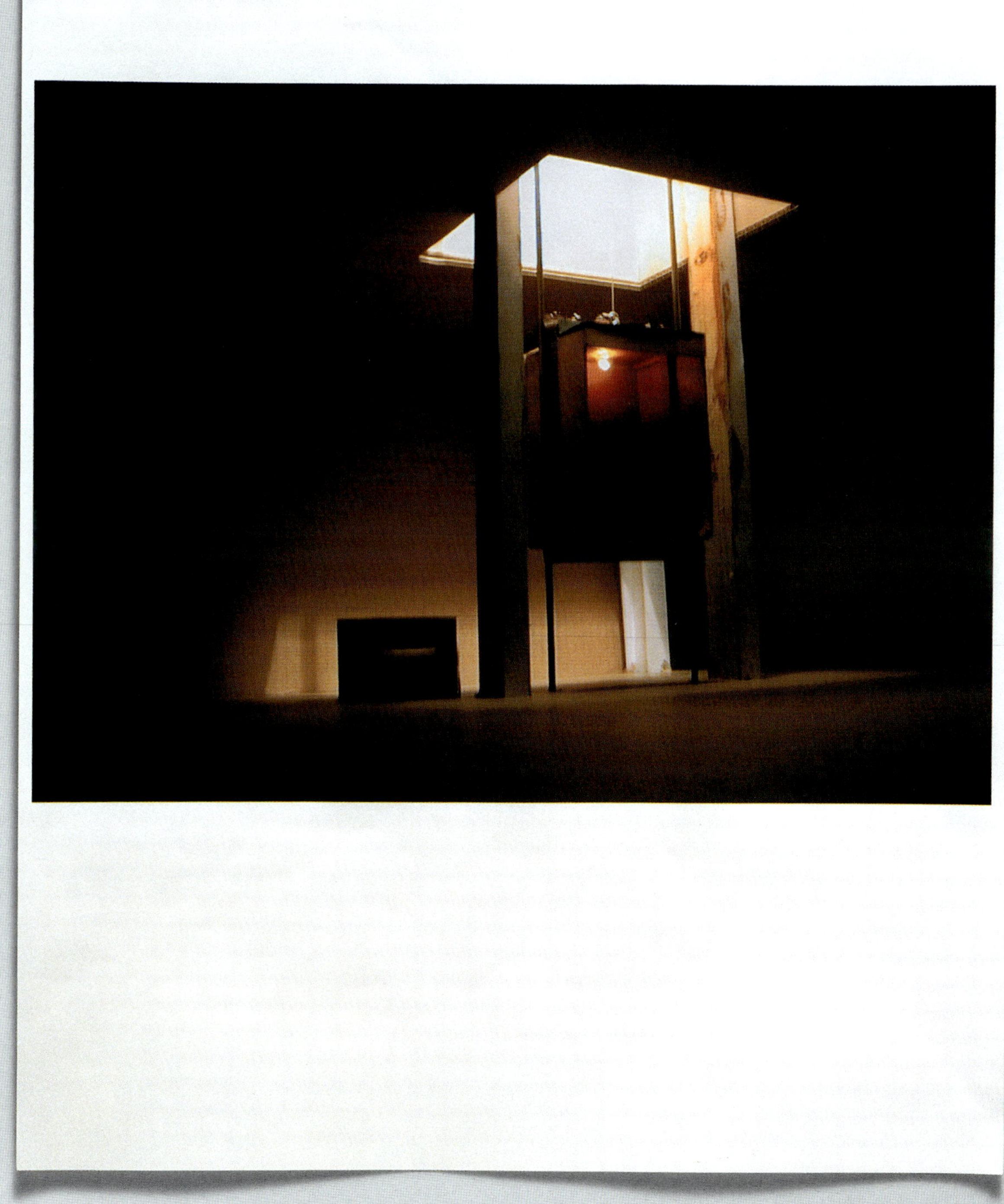

GERICAULT

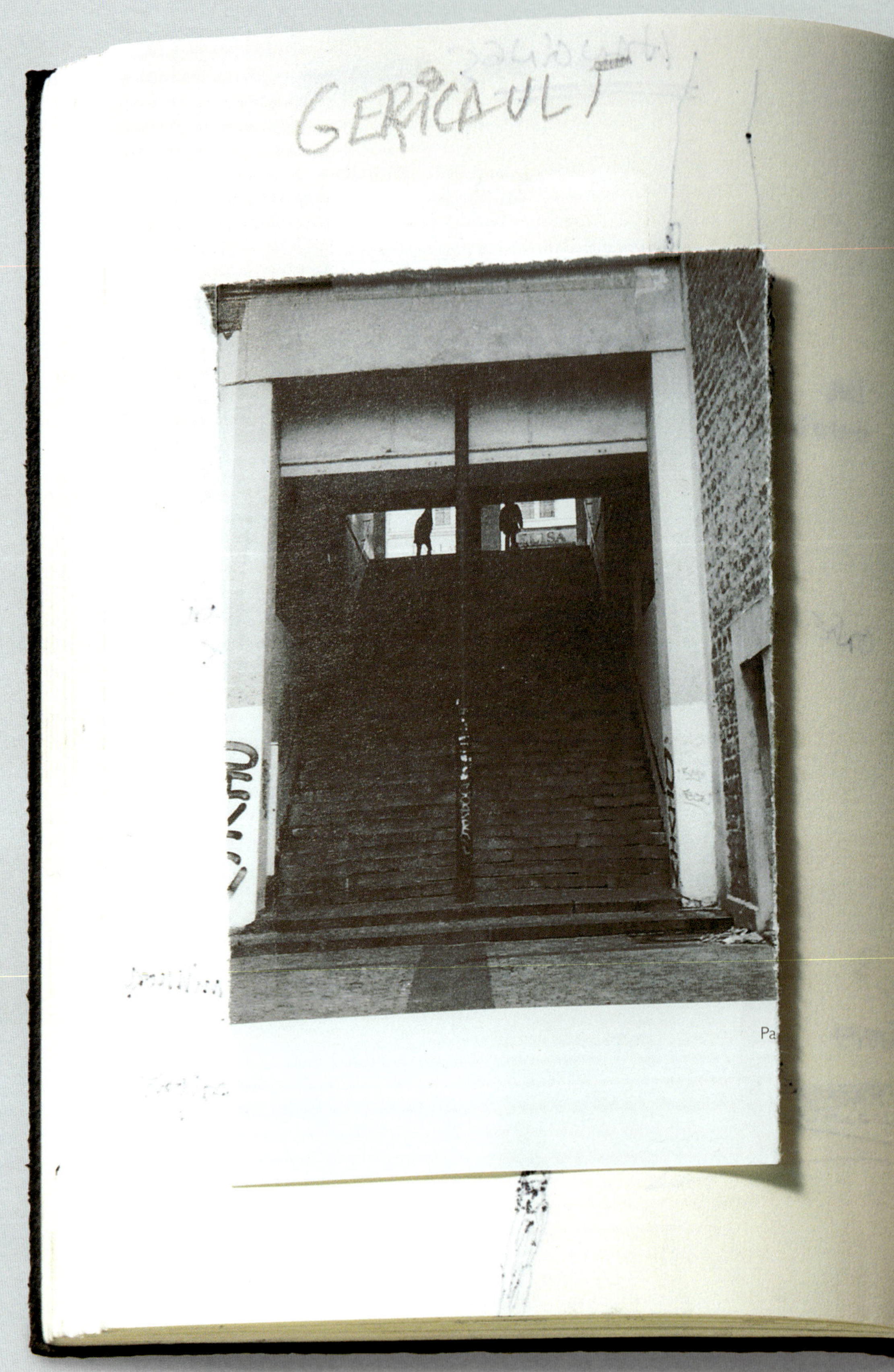

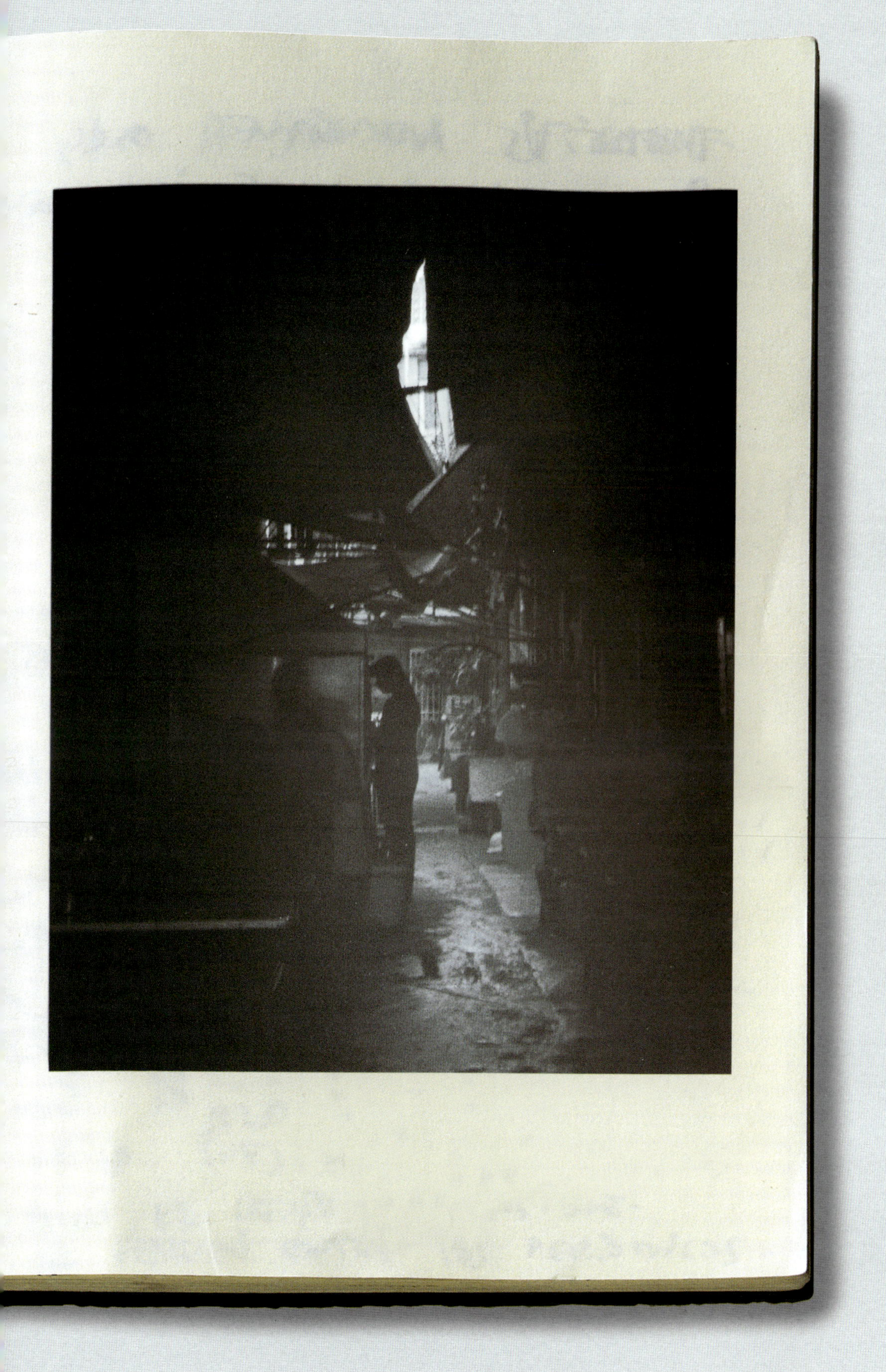

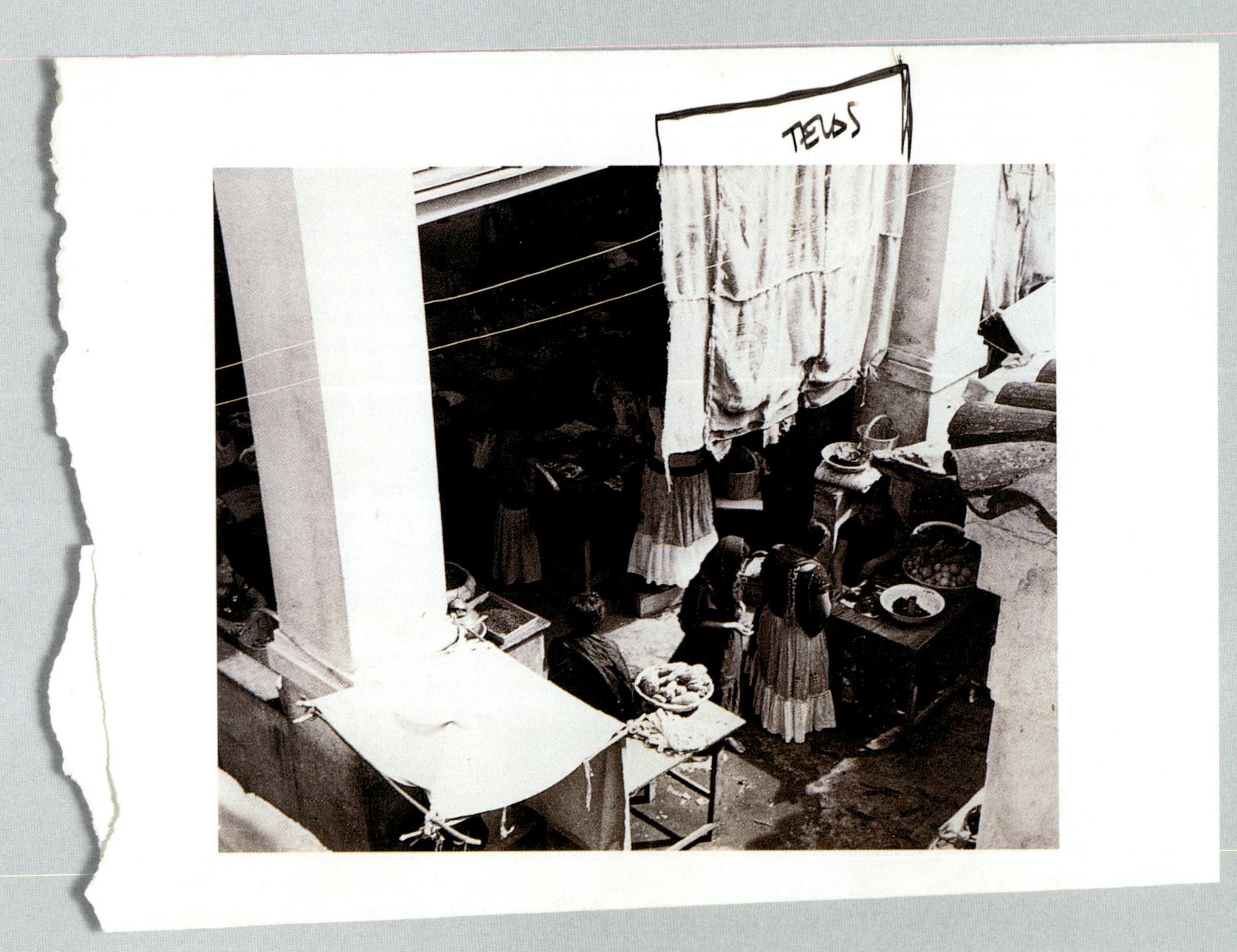
TELOS

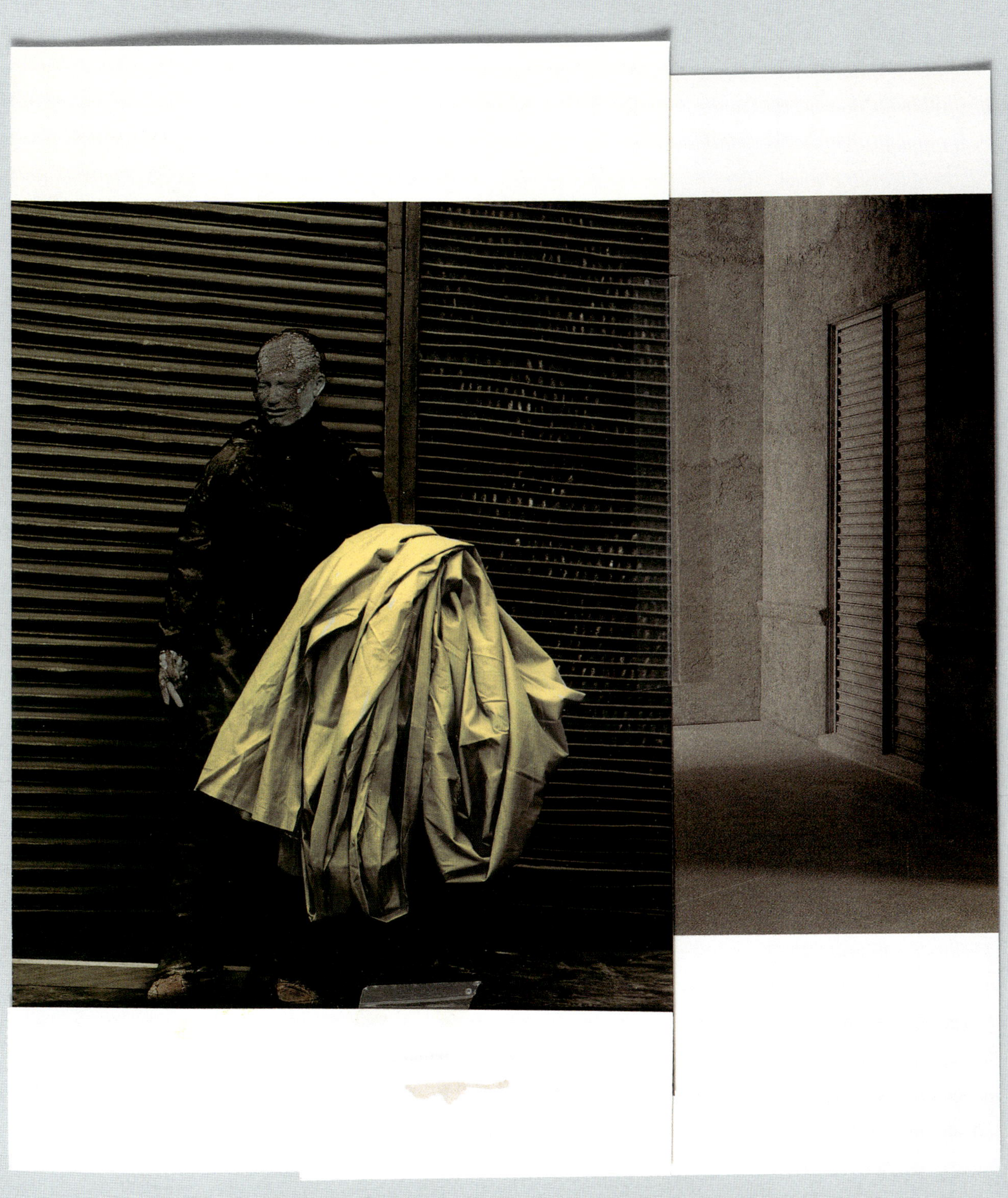

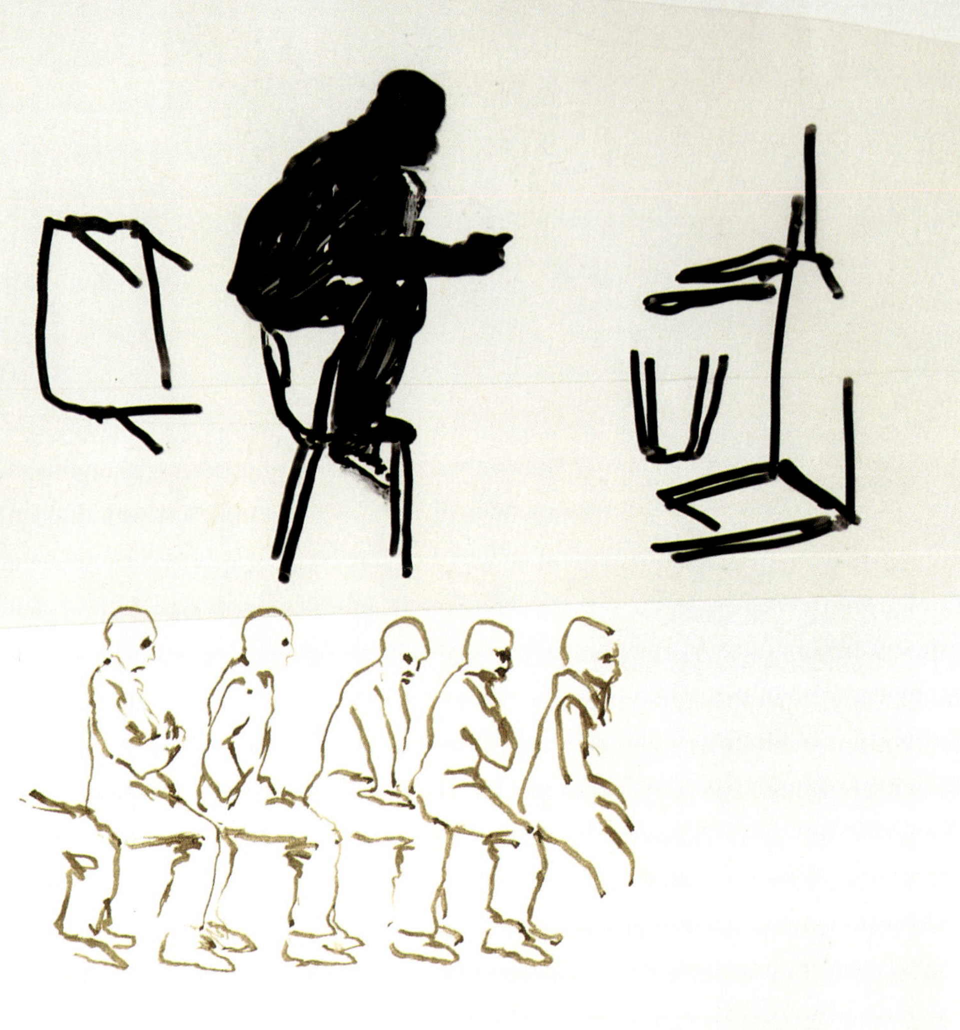

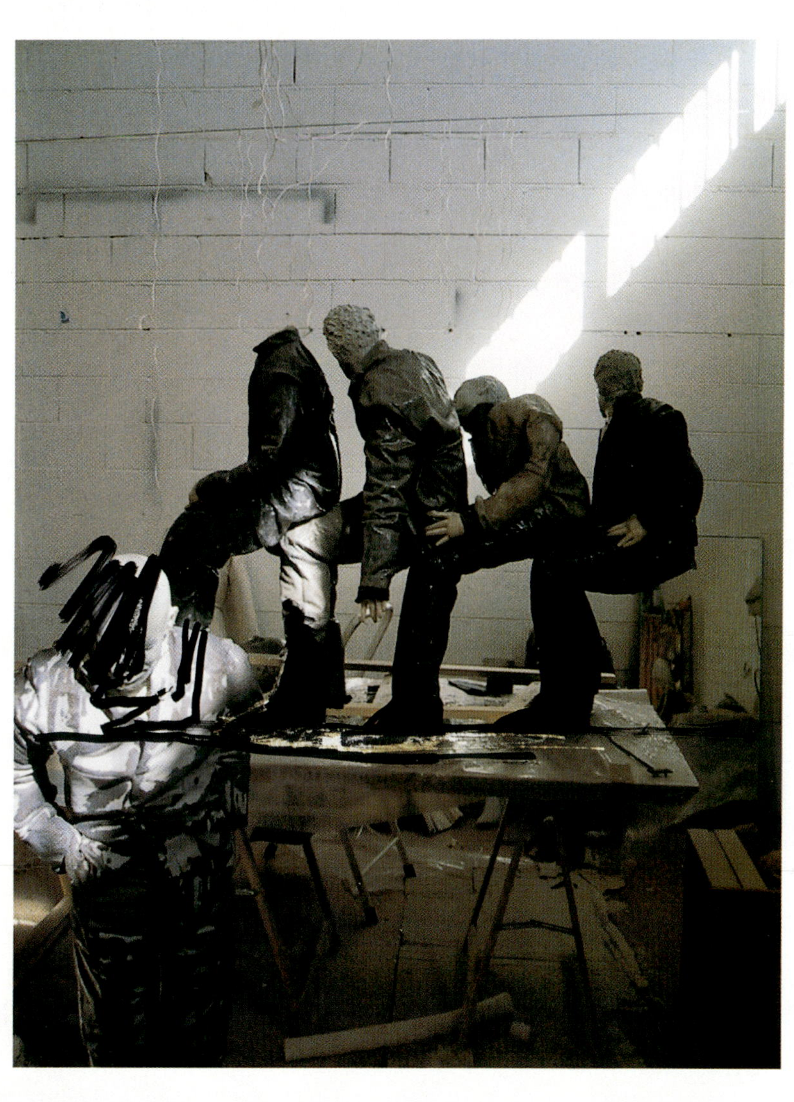

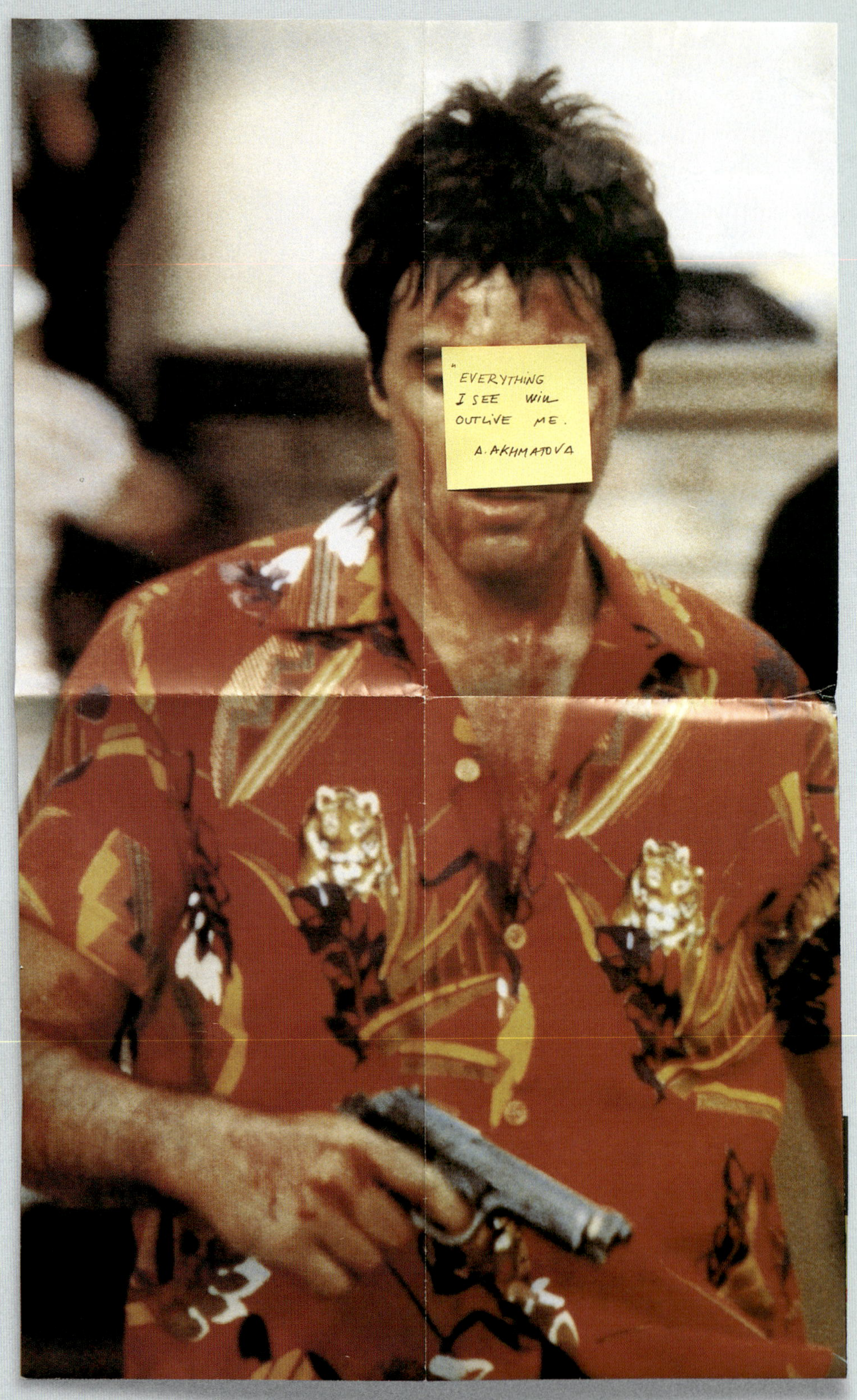
"EVERYTHING
I SEE WILL
OUTLIVE ME.
A. AKHMATOVA

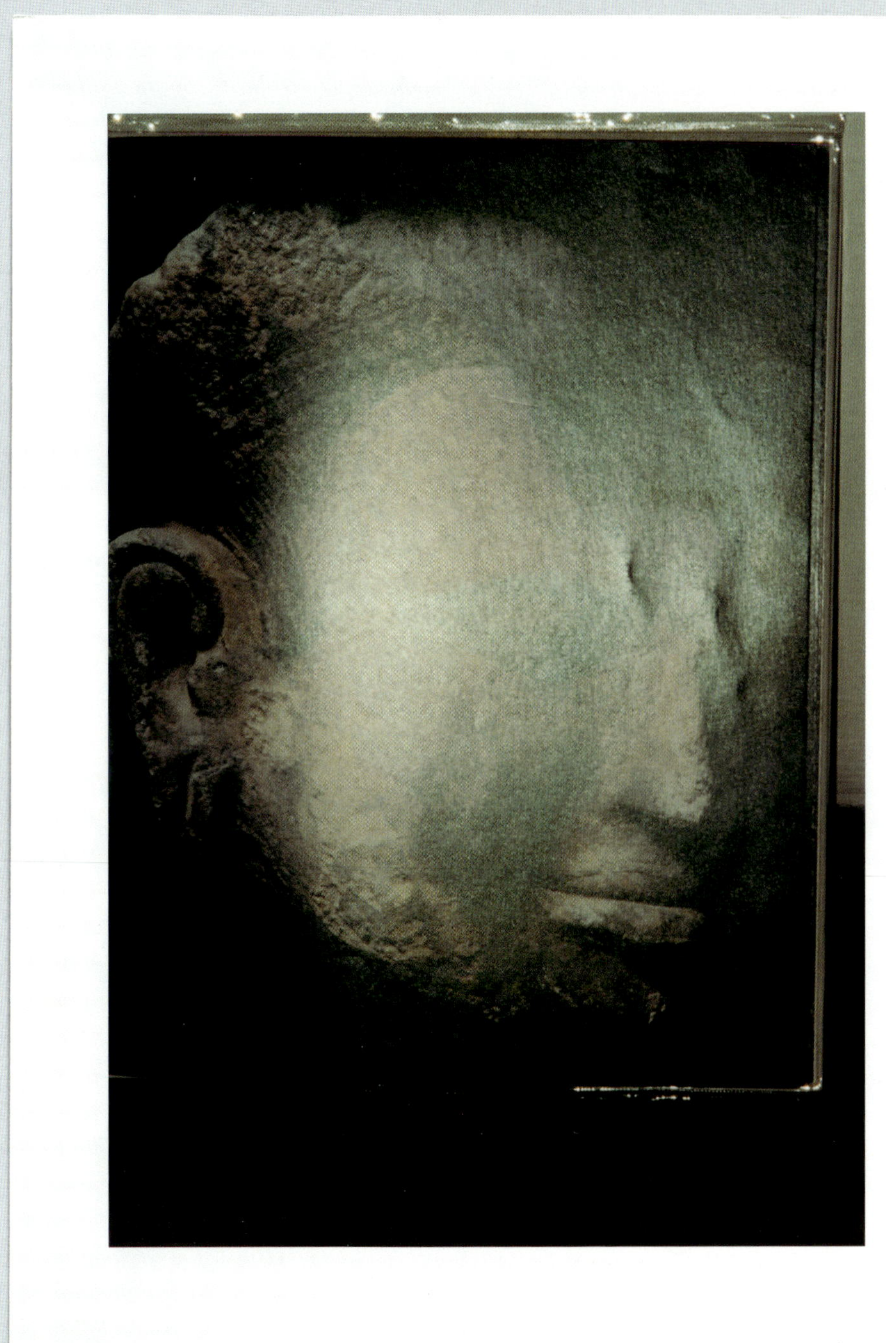

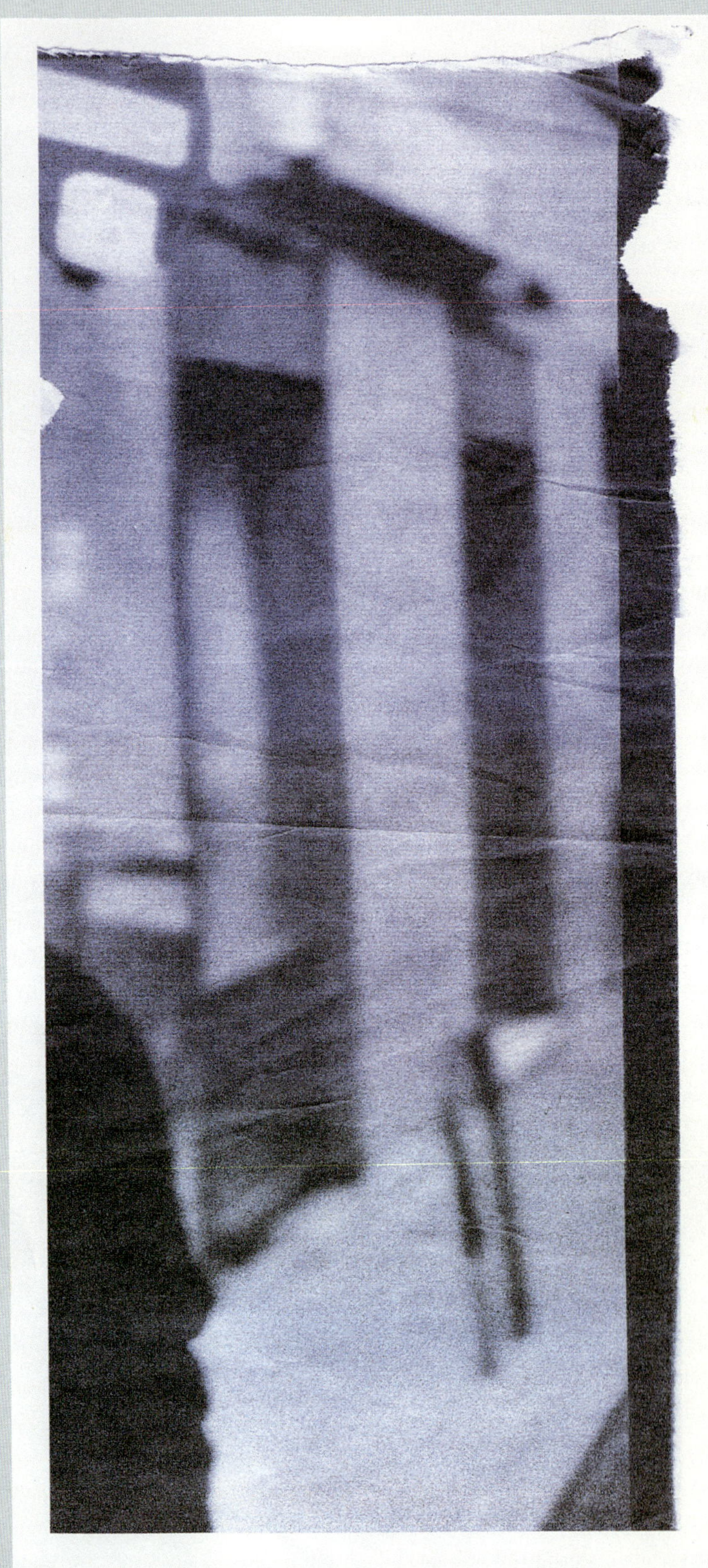

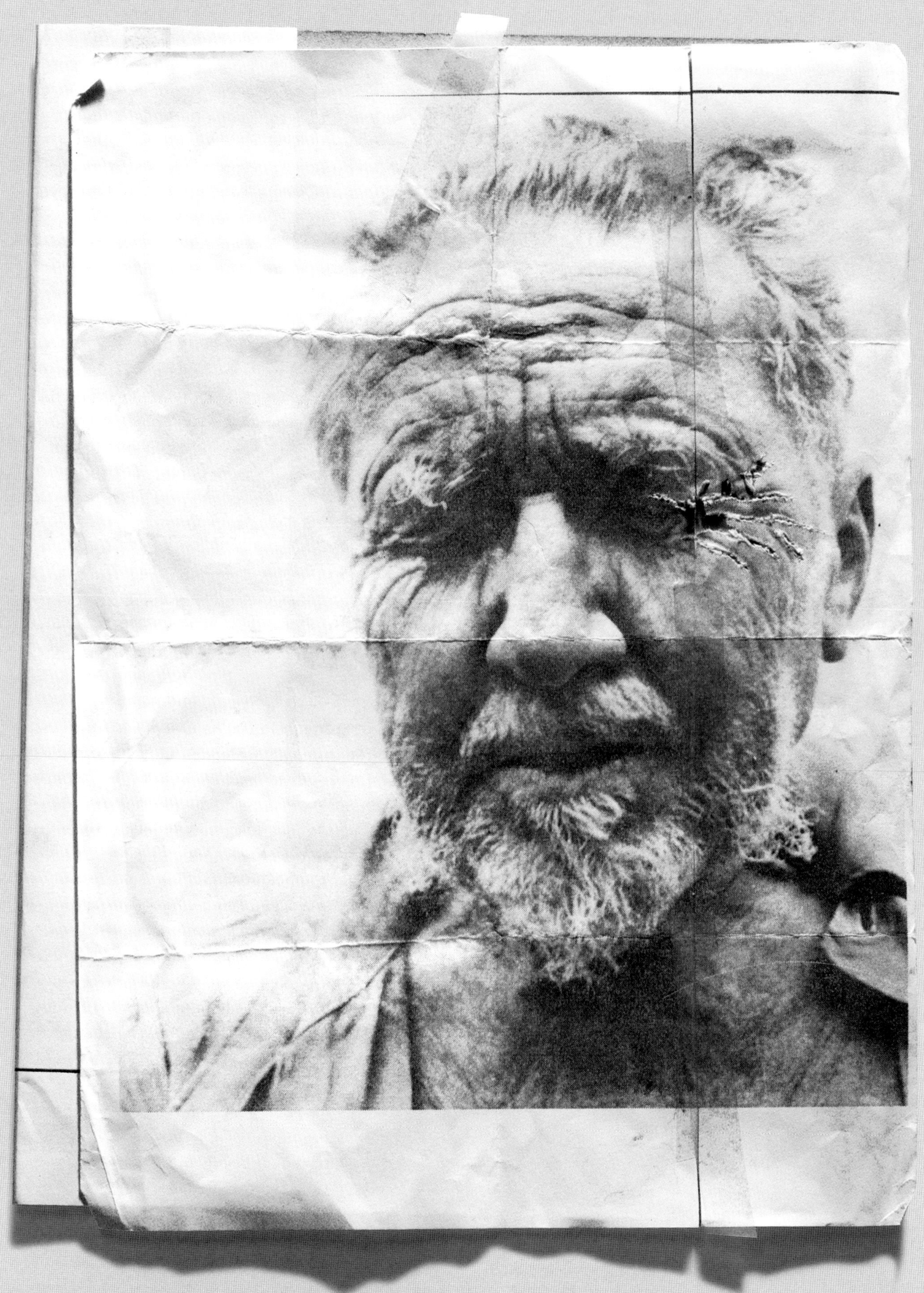

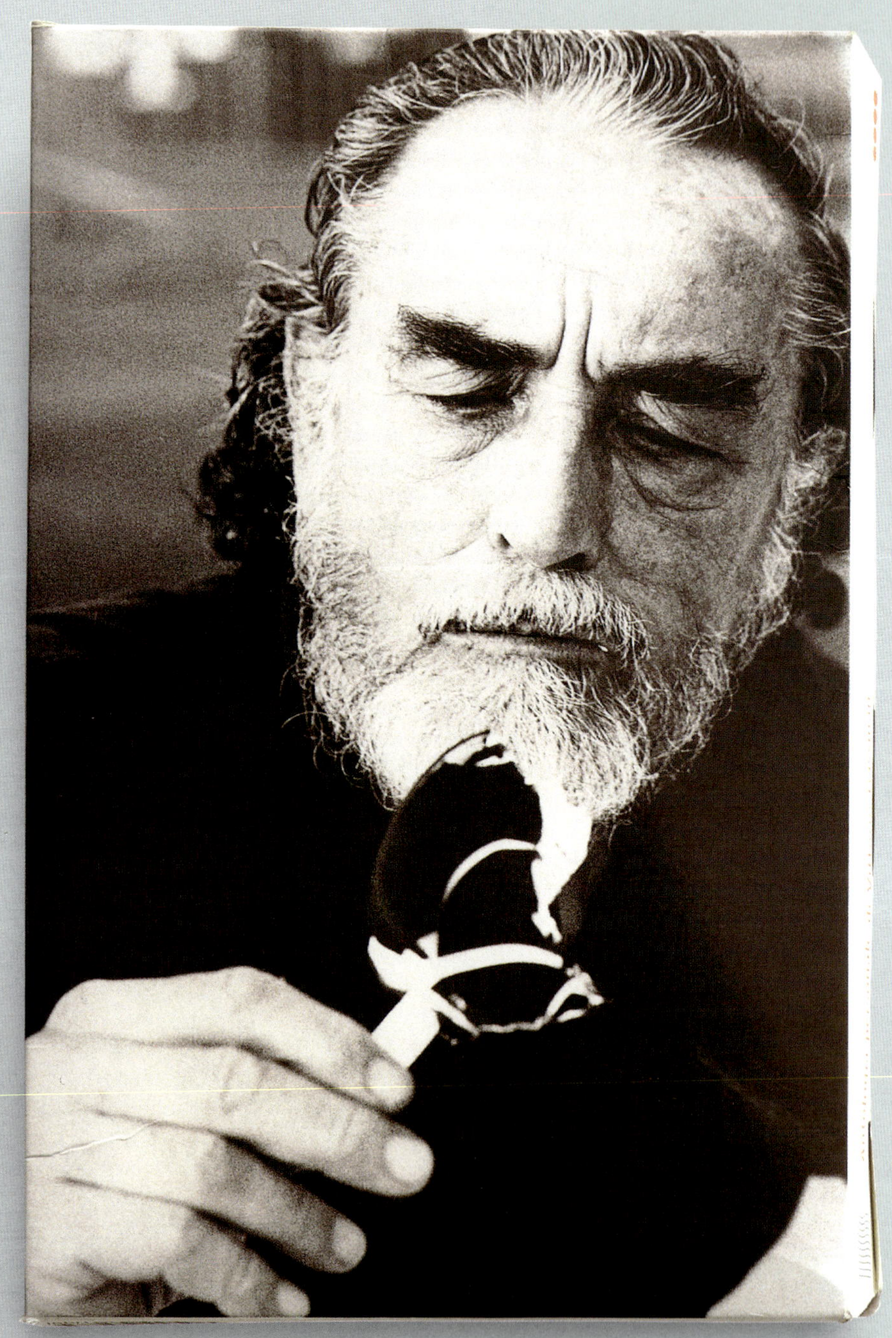

Patterns of Behaviour

SUSAN MAY

The line is made up of an infinite number of points; the plane
of an infinite number of lines; the volume of an infinite number
of planes; the hypervolume of an infinite number of volumes …
No, unquestionably this is not – more geometrico – the best
way of beginning my story. To claim that it is true is nowadays
the convention of every made-up story. Mine, however, is true.

JORGE LUIS BORGES, *The Book of Sand* [1]

In Borges's fantastical tale, the author conjures the image of a book with an incalculable number of pages. He calls it *The Book of Sand*, 'because neither the book nor the sand has any beginning or end'. [2] The narrator assures the reader that his encounter with this mysterious book was a genuine, recent event, and not simply the construct of his imagination. And yet, to accept the veracity of his account, the reader must suspend all preconceived notions of the logical and rational world.

Employing the skills of a master storyteller, the Spanish artist Juan Muñoz takes the viewer on a similar journey. Weaving fictive scenarios that embrace both the quotidian and the exceptional, his work is simultaneously appealing and dislocating. His installations implicate the audience within complex and articulate *mise-en-scènes* that transgress the divide between subject and object. The choreography of space and objects entice the spectator into an almost participatory role, immersed within a field of possibilities.

Muñoz's early sculptures of the 1980s featured architectural elements divorced of function. Balconies, unpeopled and perched inaccessibly high on the gallery walls, redundant bannisters and handrails serving no apparent purpose presented an element of uncertainty, a theme that is evident in much of the artist's work. In *First Bannister* 1987, an open flick-knife is attached to the back of the handrail, the dual connotations of which intrigued Muñoz: 'I was very interested in the idea of this work, inviting your hand to go out, and then the idea of danger.' [3] These sculptures, whose commonplace attributes belie their unpredictable nature, indirectly suggested the corresponding characteristics of walking and stability. This led to works incorporating complex patterned floors. *The Wasteland* 1987, for example, unified the sculpture of a figure in the far corner within the totality of the space. The floor's pattern served as an optical illusion, designed to confound expectations of what is set before the eye. Whilst drawing on the narrative of the barren landscape scarred by war evoked in T. S. Eliot's literary masterpiece, the work recalls other motifs from the poem:

> A current under sea
> Picked his bones in whispers.
> As he rose and fell
> He passed the stages of age and youth
> Entering the whirlpool.[4]

As one draws closer to the mute figure sitting implacably on a shelf, the floor seems to undulate. The fixed grin of the ventriloquist's dummy is as demonic and relentless as the maelstrom of pattern that has brought us to it.

A wide cast of estranged protagonists inhabit Muñoz's installations, all of whom embody a sense of quiescence and concealment. Ballerinas, rendered in bronze and weighted by solid spherical bases, are denied the opportunity to dance, left paralysed in permanent, frustrated silence. The dwarf, a figure whose artistic antecedents feature in paintings by Diego Velázquez and the films of Luis Buñuel, appears in Muñoz's work as a cipher for discomfort and the idea of 'otherness'.[5] In *The Prompter* 1988, the dwarf is located within a stage setting, with only the lower half of his body visible, forever locked in taciturn anticipation. *Dublin Dwarf* 1989, stands immutable and alone at the end of a long corridor, at once beseeching and repelling the viewer's hesitant approach.

Muñoz's figures are characterised by a shrewd indifference: they attract with their physicality, whilst remaining psychologically remote and ultimately dismissive of our presence. Their silence becomes oppressive, serving as a metaphor for the inadequacies of language and communication. The *Conversation Piece* sculptures of the early 1990s saw individuals replaced by groups of figures, absorbed in some kind of secret communion. Positioned on rotund bases, scattered throughout the space, they conduct a subtle exchange of gesticulations and covert glances, indecipherable to all but themselves. Excluded from their communications, the audience is reminded of the fundamental isolation of the human condition. In *Plaza* 1996, the number of figures was increased further, this time modelled with abbreviated 'oriental' facial characteristics and dress. They occupy the space as they might congregate within any civic square, engaged in convivial banter. But again, the sense of separateness and disjunction is palpable, rendered by the expulsion of certain individuals from the main assembly. The dynamic of relationships is nuanced by the merest adjustment in the positioning of the figures, transforming the gaps and vacant spaces into elements as critical as the objects themselves.

In 1996 and 1997, Muñoz produced two large-scale installations, the first at the Dia Center for the Arts in New York, the second at Site Santa Fe.[6] For both works the artist created a chromatically muted streetscape that adopted some of the physical and culturally specific aspects of the gallery space and its locale. A shuttered doorway or closed window, details drawn from nearby buildings, reappeared in the walls flanking the 'street' constructed within the gallery. A vocabulary of architectural signs and devices established spaces that led the spectator through seemingly abandoned alleys and uninhabited street corners. Into this landscape, which remained both recognisable and unknown, interior spaces were introduced, occupied by solitary figures, or small groups engaged in hushed and private dialogue. Each scene left the visitor more uncertain and cautious of what would confront them around the next corner, as long shadows, cast throughout the terrain, underscored a latent sense of apprehension. A number of the conceptual and physical concerns of this sequence of tableaux preface the new work made for Tate Modern. In both cases, one is somehow left with the disquieting sense of having stumbled into an unfurling drama in which one has no part. Once again, Muñoz's deft sleight of hand paradoxically combined the uncanny with the familiar, absence with occupancy, and charged silence with malevolent tension.

Muñoz was invited to make a proposal for a sculpture for the Turbine Hall at Tate Modern in February 2000. The space, which measures 152 metres in length, 24 metres in width and reaches a height of 30 metres, offers a number of challenges for the presentation of art, both in the face of its immense scale and the powerful architectural presence of Herzog and de Meuron's design within Gilbert Scott's original building. Commentators have noted how entering the Turbine Hall can be analogous to the experience of entering a cathedral.[7] From the west entrance into the building, the long ramp leading down accentuates the sweeping altitude of the space, as the eye is drawn up to the skylights and to the wall at the far end, where one might almost expect to find an altar. The ramp levels out at the foot of a staircase, which ascends to a bridge platform, bisecting the length and breadth of the Turbine Hall. To the east of the Hall, the vertical elevations of the walls and windows compete with the horizontal planes of the 'light-box' balconies and glass roof, emphasising the sheer volume of the space. Resisting the impulse to tackle this massive area by producing objects amplified to a monumental scale, Muñoz investigated more architectonic strategies to deal with the verticality and volume of the Turbine Hall. He was mindful too of how the act of looking, as a primarily individual experience, has become attenuated in modern society, and began seeking ways in which to reinvest this singular encounter in such a public space.

Returning to the Turbine Hall's correspondence with the architecture of worship, Muñoz considered the proportions and positioning of the altar within a church, high and out of reach. It draws the congregation's eye heavenwards, away from secular distractions, and intensifies the emotional response to its iconography. A primary aim was to create a work that encourages a private, subjective connection with the object, making the viewer feel as if they are completely alone with the work.[8] To engender this response in an area as vast and populated as the Turbine Hall, the artist looked for ways to enable solitary encounters, whilst addressing the spatial articulation of the work as a whole. This intention shares some of the concerns of Baroque art and architecture of the seventeenth and eighteenth centuries, points of reference for Muñoz not only in this, but also in previous works. The architectural principles of this period drew attention towards a central axis and up to the ceiling, where artists depicted the infinite, directing the viewer away from the everyday towards the divine. Emphasis was placed on illusory and dynamic compositions, blurring the distinction between the real and imaginary, and between the architectural and painted space. Muñoz has subtly explored a number of these ideas in *Double Bind*.

He chose to exploit the vertiginous height of the Turbine Hall and address the volumetric challenges of the space head on. The work proposes a variety of visual riddles which play on perspective, illusion, visibility and invisibility. Approaching the work from the west entrance, one's attention is immediately drawn to a dramatic intervention within the space, signalled by the distant view of two narrow steel structures, scaling the ceiling of the hall. Climbing and descending these supports at varying speeds are two elevator cars, bearing no passengers and apparently locked in perpetual motion. Drawn towards the kinetics of the elevators, the visitor is faced with two options: to continue their journey at ground level, or to ascend the stairs to the overhead bridge to gain a better view. Selecting the latter, the spectator arrives at the top of the stairs to be confronted by an array of visual conundrums. What was once a bridge has metamorphosed into a gateway heralding a patterned floor, extending the length and breadth of the east end of the Turbine Hall. The handrail, a relic of the former bridge, denies passage onto this floor, reiterating a motif of previous works – the thresholds between performer and audience, viewer and viewed, past and present. The surface floor pattern features a series of 'holes', or 'shafts', indicating the abyss below. The ambiguous status of these – as actual voids or illusory spaces rendered on the surface – calls to mind the dissolve between the real and the represented as exercised by practitioners of the Baroque. The deployment of optical illusion in the *trompe l'oeil* design emphasises depth of perspective. As if drawing on a Kantian account of the mathematical sublime, the space appears overwhelmingly vast. Large black shafts at the front contract into shadowy fissures at the farthest point from the viewing platform, and the alignment of pattern draws the eye to the dramatic action of the elevators, as they puncture through the floor, rupturing the illusion of a single, solid plain.

The momentum of the elevators seems to echo the constant movement occurring within the Turbine Hall, with its steady flow of visitors perambulating through the space. Viewed from the platform bridge, ant-like figures meander up and down the wide ramp from the entrance. Looking up from the ground floor affords the viewer a glimpse of individuals passing by at different levels, of groups strolling along the bridge, and torsos momentarily bending over the balustrade. The differing speeds of the elevators' journey are in concert with this state of flux, acting as a parallel to the changing pace of the visitors' peregrinations.

By disappearing through the floor, the elevators direct attention to the space below. Descending the stairs to ground level, the atmosphere registers a darker tone, or, as aptly described by the artist, evinces a 'subterranean emotion'.[9] The architectural accoutrements beneath the original bridge platform – the supporting steel I-beams, the staggered fluorescent tracks attached to the ceiling – are replicated within the space, making the existing structure coalesce with the new. Advancing into this relatively compressed chamber is akin to walking through an underground car park, an arena that is, in cinema and television at least, shorthand for impending danger, with murky shadows, disembodied footsteps and screeching tyres. Moving on, the artificial lighting peters out, casting the viewer into darkness, to become accustomed to the tenebrous environment, which is imbued with a sense of foreboding and ambiguity. As the art historian Anthony Vidler has noted, such 'space is assumed to hide, in its darkest recesses and forgotten margins, all objects of fear and phobia that have returned with such insistency to haunt the imaginations of those who have tried to stake out spaces to protect their health and happiness'.[10]

Deprived of light and offered little indication of where this journey may lead, the observer's sensory perception is intensified, as if one is cautiously wandering through a darkened room before the lights are switched on, attempting to anticipate what might be encountered along the way. The viewer becomes part of the space and the space becomes part of the viewer. The physical sense of being is enhanced to such a degree as to almost become an 'out of body' experience. As architectural historian Richard Etlin has observed: 'At the deepest end of the aesthetic scale, in situations to which we attach the notion of the sublime, it is the spatial sense of self that is most directly engaged in a pantheistic feeling of transport and transcendence.'[11] Dimly, through the maze of supporting columns, the animation and hum of the elevators is discernible. Providing a concrete connection with the space overhead, to be viewed in conjunction with other strategic features such as the open shafts, the elevators offer clues to establish a topographical landscape that may relate the view from above to the space at ground level. However, further analysis reveals that the configuration of open shafts does not read true in relation to the surface design. Apertures signified above ground fail to reappear below, whilst pockets of diffused light fall from just a handful of 'real' shafts.

Perplexed by such deceiving evidence, and still unable to circumscribe the totality of the space, the curious viewer arrives at illuminated pools falling from the shafts overhead. At this point, signs of inhabitance are signalled. Architectural elements, shuttered windows and air-conditioning units located within the walls of the shafts indicate proof of occupancy. A sense of surveillance begins to register. Perched within the balcony spaces, small groups of sculpted figures are assembled, some looking down, others absorbed in surreptitious and ambiguous exchanges. Looking up, the viewer is forced to pay attention, to become immersed in the act of seeing, a fact taken into consideration by Muñoz when addressing the challenge 'to make a work that individualises the experience of the spectator'.[12] Art-historical

parallels are called to mind, from Giambattista Tiepolo's swiftly rendered,
foreshortened figures peering down from a carefully arranged architectural
framework, to the dynamic use of oblique perspective as seen in the photographic
innovations of Aleksandr Rodchenko.[13] With attention focused on the figures,
a sense of the psychological condition of unease and anxiety grows in the dawning
recognition of having been placed in a position of vulnerability. The role of
subject/performer is supplanted, with Muñoz's figures becoming spectators,
insouciantly glancing down or turning away from their elevated position.
Squinting at the light, the meaning of their quizzical expressions remains
unclear, as does the primary purpose of their attendance in the interstices of the
chamber. Lone figures stand in contemplation, whilst others scurry away into
the void beyond, into a virtual city hidden from the spectator's view.

The visitor's migration through the sculpture eventually reaches the edge
of the space, where they must turn and retrace their steps, passing under the
watchful eye of the figures. Moving back and forth between the shafts, a different
tale emerges from each, with protagonists involved in situations that somehow
elude total comprehension, like a collection of short stories that build into
an enigmatic whole.

1 Jorge Luis Borges, *The Book of Sand*, London 1971, p.87.
2 Ibid., p.89.
3 James Lingwood, *Juan Muñoz: Monologues and Dialogues*, Museum für Gegenwartskunst, Zurich 1997, p.59.
4 *The Wasteland* (IV 'Death by Water') in T. S. Eliot, *Collected Poems 1909–1962*, London 1974, p.75.
5 'I was not so interested in the physical presence of the dwarf. It was more a reference to the question of strangeness than the problem of size.' From 'A Conversation, New York, 22 January 1995, Juan Muñoz and James Lingwood', *Parkett*, no. 43, 1995, p.42.
6 See Lynne Cooke, 'Juan Muñoz', *A Place Called Abroad and Streetwise*, exh. cat., Dia Center for the Arts, New York 1999.
7 See Rowan Moore and Raymund Ryan, *Building Tate Modern*, London 2000.
8 Muñoz has commented on his aim to create work that elicits an equivalent sensation to that of 'standing alone, still and silent, in a darkened room'. He has also noted that the 'best moments of looking are when you're the only one looking'. Discussion with the author, 20 March 2000.
9 Discussion with the author, 2 October 2000.
10 Anthony Vidler, *The Architectural Uncanny*, Cambridge, Mass. 1992, p.167.
11 Richard Etlin, 'Aesthetics and the Spatial Sense of Self', *The Journal of Aesthetics and Art Criticism*, 56:1, Winter 1998, p.1.
12 Discussion with the author, 2 October 2000.
13 *Monologues and Dialogues*, op. cit., p.39. See also Magdalena Dabrowski, Leah Dickerman, Peter Galassi, *Aleksandr Rodchenko*, exh. cat., Museum of Modern Art, New York, 1998.

A Conversation, May 2001

JUAN MUÑOZ AND JAMES LINGWOOD

JL How much of this project was latent in your mind before you were invited to work in the Turbine Hall?

JM I don't think it is possible to have anything waiting in your imagination for a space and a volume of this kind. The space is there, it's a given. Then I have my language and my experience, that's it. These are the starting points. I don't think anybody can really shape a work like this prior to being asked. You have to come, to look, to despair and smile.

JL Had you seen the space before Tate Modern opened?

JM I saw it before it was open to the public. I saw it empty, which is maybe important.

JL What were the first ideas that you envisaged? Were they close to what you're finally going to make here?

JM I don't think I had an immediate vision in front of the space. I did spend many days walking up and down but I could not envisage anything. I did what I believe many artists probably do, and walked through endless amounts of books, and through the streets, taking in all of the little incidents and accidents and encounters of everyday life. You hope that images will resonate in your mind and that they will help to lead you on, to find some shape and form to begin with.

JL Which images began to resonate?

JM My first idea, or image if you like, was to build two successive bridges. I don't know why – it just came in a very intuitive way: two bridges tilted into the horizon, disappearing into the distance. There was a photograph of two bridges in Ljubljana that I found very interesting on a spatial level. That was the very first idea: standing on a bridge – or a plateau – and looking at something that was leading nowhere; a bridge from nowhere to nowhere. My second idea was to suspend a great number of figures in the space. These are some of what I would call the habitual errors along the way.

JL Maybe there's a key consideration here already – the tension between creating an image and building a sculpture. The two bridges could have worked beautifully as an image but you want people to move around the space, and to experience the work in a way that's not just about surveying a kind of landscape.

JM   No, that should only be one dimension of the work. Somehow, I think it became important for me not to repeat myself. I might have achieved a powerful effect by approximating the project I made in Copenhagen last year with 120 figures installed on a huge balcony, or by doing something similar to the circle of Chinese figures at the Velázquez Palace in Madrid: not allowing people to walk in but to see it only from above. But it's important not to stand still.

JL   Did the idea of figures suspended in a space mean that you felt you had to address the verticality? Because you've transformed large horizontal expanses before – such as in Madrid or in the courtyard in Dublin. In Dublin you looked across the space, and perhaps down onto it, but you didn't need to address the problem of looking up.

JM   The verticality of the Turbine Hall is extreme. I am sure that in the final installation it will give me problems that I cannot imagine now.

JL   Maybe you only have two possibilities – to keep very close to the ground – as many sculptors have done since the 1960s, or somehow to engage with the verticality. The horizontal expanse isn't so intimidating.

JM   It is true that the horizontality was never the biggest challenge. You can talk about verticality in formal terms but also in symbolic terms. The verticality of the hanging figures that I started to think about in the beginning was certainly a way of dealing with the gigantic distortion that happens when you look up. Probably the image of the elevator that came later on is a resolution of how to engage with the verticality.

JL   But without providing a fixed image. The fact that there's a slow motion through the space is significant – particularly because the rest of the landscape is still.

JM   Actually, one of the many momentary images I had as an idea for intersecting the space was of a suspended carpet – with people above it, and people below

it. But then the cut would just have been a horizontal one, not a vertical one.
The associations weren't right, but anyway it pushed me towards the idea
of having two separate spatial experiences, above and below. So the carpet
evolved into a floor. This gives two quite different kinds of space – and the
dialectic between the two is important.

JL   A space you could survey but not walk through, and a space that you could
walk through but not survey, and the elevators linking the overground to
the underworld ?

JM   I remember talking to you some months ago about installing several elevators,
and then sensing the inappropriate excess, so I reduced the number of
elevators to three, and then to two. The idea of the duet began to shape the
thinking.

JL   When you work with figurative motifs – and the elevators imply figures,
even if there are no figures within these ones – you again have a spectrum of
possibilities: the solitary figure, the duet, the small group or conversation,
or the crowd. Would more than two elevators have created too much of a
performance, a concerto of automated movement?

JM   Trying now to reconstruct how the piece came about, it's difficult because
I don't clearly remember how the final form was determined – and there are
still many, many decisions to be made. We certainly talked about several
elevators being too many, and then three seemed a good idea, with one of
them broken and two of them travelling; and then two seemed right, and
this brought a kind of musical discourse to the discussion, the idea of a duet,
and this started to frame the subject. Because there *was* no subject before the
horizontality, and the verticality – the formal problems began to lead towards
the subject. I'm trying to remember the nights and the wine and the
conversations. Many decisions are shaped by an accidental encounter, by
hearing or seeing something unexpected. The moment when my wife
Cristina [the artist Cristina Iglesias] said that coming down the ramp at
Tate Modern made her feel as if she were going into a parking lot was
important. It's surprising how slowly the piece started shaping itself, from
the horizontality of the bridges, to the need to deal with the verticality through
the hanging figures, which was later substituted by the absence of the figures,

to the displacement of these ideas with others that seemed more complete
and more economical.

J L   This is a familiar process in your work – from having various scenarios or
ideas that gradually get pared down, the image of a human presence is
displaced by the idea of absence, or emptiness. The balconies in some of
your very first sculptures were filled with representations, then they became
empty. Do you consciously build things up so that you can then take them
away again?

J M   It's not a systematic, conscious method, no. But in this particular case, in the
studio, I spend more time destroying than constructing.

J L   What kind of metaphorical function do the elevators have?

J M   They aren't metaphors for anything. They are elevators going up and down.

J L   But automated movement has been important in some of your earlier works.
I'm thinking of the figures in a shoe-box going round and round
a room on tracks. They're just stuck in their box, going round.

J M   I have often given myself fairly limited areas to work with – the problem of the
statuary for example – and asked myself how to make something significant
today within these limits. On the one hand there is the stillness of a figurative
sculpture that for me remains an inexplicable enigma. On the other hand, the
representation of movement and gesture within stillness is a challenge that
is endlessly fascinating. And the idea of a sculpture that moves, from the
Jewish notion of the golem onwards, can create a moment of wonder. The
elevators encapsulate movement, but in a suffocating way. I think between
the stillness and the movement I try to find a place for my sculptures.

J L   The elevators just endlessly go up and down in the same way that the figures
in the shoe-box go round and round.

J M   It happens that the world as I know it obliges me to go back again and
again to a circular condition. But it does not mean that I do not want to
break the circularity.

J L   What does this circularity mean? It's a strong motif in modernist art – think
of Duchamp's rotoreliefs for example. They change but never change.

JM I understand this emotion so well, this Duchampian moment of make-believe, this spinning wheel that makes you feel for a split second as if you are looking into a vacuum. The moment you switch it off, it disappears. The relationship of the flatness of the relief, and the awareness of the trick is critical. That is at the core of some of the best art of our time: the awareness of how things are done colliding with the way things appear. The making is fundamental to the illusion it creates. It is very surprising how we want to see something that does not exist.

JM It's still very intuitive, because you are talking to me about a sculpture that is yet to be made, but I'm beginning to look at the Turbine Hall as part of a city rather than part of a museum. It's a fragment of the urban experience. I'm interested in creating an urban work with several strata: a street full of doors for someone walking down the corridor hoping no door will open before the one he wants to open.

JM I'm not interested in scenography. It is a sculpture that includes other sculptures, and several viewpoints. This kind of anonymous space, a sort of extended underground like a car park, is very familiar to us all. It is a space of our time. It is never night-time and never day-time. It's identical at 11.00 in the morning and 3.00 at night and it could be almost anywhere in the world. These kinds of architectural spaces are very recent. They are a condition of our modernity. They are as quintessential as television and probably they became a common experience in our culture at around the same time.

JM Yes, nothing has been added to them. For me, perhaps it's this lack of identity that makes them so interesting. But they are still emotionally loaded, even if they are anonymous. The important thing is that they are spaces of transition, of passage, to be used and then abandoned. No-one stays for longer than they need to. No-one seems to own them, there is no sense of responsibility for them, no desire to make them more than they are. They just exist down there.

JL You're playing with different perceptual and experiential modes. You have one very classical viewing position – a view from a bridge, standing at the threshold and looking out over a scene in front of you. And then you've juxtaposed this with a different kind of experience – the experience unfolds in a different way, it unfolds in time. And then there's a third space – the interstitial space.

JM This is probably the most difficult part of the space to articulate. Of all the times I have worked before, on big projects such as the Palacio de Velázquez in Madrid or at the DIA Foundation in New York, this is the space about which I know the least. This in-between space will hopefully counterbalance the other two.

JL You were saying that you hope the viewer will experience this work as they might experience being in a city rather than being in a museum.

JM Working on this project I have become more aware even than I wish to be about the role of the spectator and his or her circulation. I know that 10,000 people are going to be there some days, and I'm trying to build a work to which they can pay attention as if they were the only one there. I'm trying to individualise the act of looking and perceiving.

JL Does looking up help individualise the act? Would you imagine your piece in the same way if there were ten spectators a day?

JM I don't think I'm building the piece for a crowd of people, I'm making the piece for one, a given person at a given time. It makes no difference to me if that person is one of 10,000 or one of ten. Probably I'm making the piece for myself and trying to make a work that I could look at as if I were not the one who made it, but as somebody else. I don't like crowded museums and being aware of other people while I'm looking at something.

JL The dynamics of looking is something you've been working on for some twenty years now – from the very first sculptures with figures in balconies, to the more complex configurations in larger spaces.

JM   I'm surprised how some of the very early ideas implied in the balconies seem
      to have reappeared in this work.

JL   Why do you think that is?

JM   I do not like to repeat myself, but sometimes I cannot help but use mechanisms
      of perception that I invented for myself and were necessary for me very early
      on. I haven't used the act of looking up so strongly since the very beginning.
      It is very strange to perceive so many years later that I'm paying so much
      attention to the act of walking through the street and looking up.

JL   The implication of looking up somehow is that someone is looking down
      at you.

JM   It's probably implicit. I hope that the elevators will create an extreme image,
      a compression of meaning, in the sense that it will accentuate all of these
      possibilities.

JL   I remember early on in your career, maybe just after you made the balconies,
      that you spent quite a lot of time in Rome. The act of looking is dramatised in
      a very strong way there, especially in some of the great Baroque churches.

JM   It takes a non-believer to construct a devotional space. That's something you
      learn in Rome. The great constructors of these interiors didn't necessarily
      believe in the conclusion at the altar.

JL   They were being asked to respond to the possibility of belief disappearing?

JM   I think that the great artists of the Baroque were being asked what modern
      artists are also being asked – to perform, to construct . . .

JL   To construct what?

JM   To construct a lie, to build a fictional place. To make the world larger than
      it is. In the Baroque period they had a multiplicity of media too. The church
      was a great cinema. You had the smells, the music, the clothing.

JL   As if they wanted to envelop the visitor, to make sure they believed. But
      you don't believe it?

JM   Sure I don't believe it. I'm the one who is painting the black hole!

J M   You don't ultimately try to transcend the physicality of experience. Being in a given room, you receive a given experience. Many good modern artists are as skilful as the great old masters of the Baroque. You learn that very well from Joseph Beuys – how you install something in a room, the apparent disdain or indifference, the pretence that it is accidental. In a Beuys room you think the things have been abandoned by the transport people, but they're very carefully placed. You believe what he wishes you to believe. Smithson, in his *Spiral Jetty*, proved to be equally as brilliant as Borromini could be. We are confronted in modern times with the task of placing and displacing objects in a given environment. It requires an understanding of the physical framework, but also of the moment of the spectator's arrival into the room. You have to make this person trust for a second that what he wishes to believe is true. And maybe you can spin that into another reality and make him wonder.

J L   The visitor to a Borromini church wanted to believe, and maybe the visitor to a Beuys performance did too. How can you think about belief today, in what is a fundamentally sceptical time?

J M   The conviction has to originate in the gaze, because now we don't believe in anything but our eyes – and very soon we're going to disbelieve them too.

J L   What do you want your spectator to believe in ?

J M   Well... to believe... it's such a difficult word. It's such a big word, it's almost excluded from ordinary speech. You know what I want? The suspension of disbelief. Even if it's a cliché, it's still relevant: to let go of what you already know, even if just for a moment. For years, as a kid, I had a private tutor called Santiago Amon who was a brilliant scholar as well as a writer on art. One afternoon, as he was showing me a book of Mondrian's paintings, he just said to me 'Drown'. I did not understand then, but he was right. That's all that you can do. Either you drown or you do not. John Berger once said that the chair of Rietveld is not a chair but an act of faith.

J L   Can you hope for a similar act of faith today?

J M   It is a very different time. Most of the time if you walk through the big museums you can see that people don't look. Or maybe they look in a different way. They walk through museums as if they were walking in a modern street, like Walter Benjamin's idea of the arcade, strolling past elegant objects that they probably could not afford to buy. They are just surrounded by these images and these moments of luxury … And you are the maker of an object and you wonder what is your role is in relation to all this.

J L Can we just go back to the Baroque for a moment. The way in which these interiors constructed the position of the spectator seemed to make their place in the hierarchy quite clear – that there was a kind of power from above that almost enveloped the people inside.

J M Yes, but there is also an important role played by the view from below. These buildings were made to provoke a centrifugal sense of direction, to create a certain disorientation, even dizziness, as you look from the floor to the ceiling.

J L The figures in your studio at the moment, will they inhabit the space in-between the floor and the ceiling?

J M My studio, like the living room of a piano player, is not the best room in which to listen to the work. So we will have to see. Right now, all the figures seem to be moving … going away.

J L There's a feeling of looking for something?

J M I remember we were sitting in your kitchen not too long ago and you asked me why I came to London in the first place, back in the 1970s, and I said I came to London to look for my brother. I did find him, and I did find a small flat to rent, and I did find a job, and I did find a language I could deal with, in order to buy food and pay the rent; and I did find a culture that allowed me to respect myself as a contemporary European.

J L Why were you looking for your brother?

J M I was looking for my brother who was looking for David Cooper, a famous psychiatrist. Cooper was part of a group of analysts, along with R. D. Laing, who were rethinking parts of Gregory Bateson's theory of the 'Double Bind' as a way of dealing with schizophrenia.

J L Is the theory of the Double Bind important to this new project?

JM   No, not really. The title of the piece came very late.

JL   If you were looking for your brother, were you also looking for yourself?
     This brings us back to the idea of the duet or the double in a way.

JM   Well, yes and no. No – it takes you to the idea of a subject. The idea of
     looking for a subject is extremely relevant. You construct the work and you
     adjust the construction to a kind of subject. With this work, I have forced
     every image to be an empty image. The elevators carry nobody. The windows
     lead nowhere. They imply the night, the closing down of the street, the
     moment of closure. Everything seems to be closed down. All of the figures
     have very tightly closed eyes.

JL   Have you been surprised that your experience in London almost thirty years
     ago has somehow come into the present work?

JM   It would be a mistake to think about this piece as a reinterpretation of
     my memory.

JL   But it's in there somewhere?

JM   If I had been asked to make this project in a museum in Berlin, or Los Angeles,
     I would not have had any personal experience, nor specific memories. I wanted
     the work to have an interior quality so I revisited the same streets, some of
     the same places I visited thirty years ago, so perhaps these memories did
     bring something to the work, help me shape it, because I am being asked
     thirty years later to perform in a city in which I grew up. On the other hand,
     I also spent some time in some cities in the Far East last year and that was
     very important too.

JL   So you have the idea of a duet, the two lifts that come up and down, and the
     two levels, and yourself and your brother. There's an exploration of identity
     here. If you were looking for anyone else except your brother, maybe it would
     be different.

JM   He came to London to look for a person. But the person whom he thought
     could help him was already an alcoholic so there was no hope. Cooper could
     not help him because he was already incapable of helping himself. The
     awareness of the impossibility does not make you any happier. You are

striving for a solution but you do not find one. There is no poetry, no beauty, no sense attached to this kind of despair. You feel there is no way out, and that shapes your identity too.

JL   Do you want to show people the emptiness?

JM   You don't show the emptiness. You show the wish for it to be full. There is nothing rewarding in emptiness, in an empty elevator. I don't look back on the balconies as empty, they are about anything but themselves. They are images that are already there, already used. The balcony, the mirror, the back of the mirror...

JL   The above and the below. The subconscious is so much bigger.

JM   Yes – for all of us. I'm so happy that you point to the subconscious. It's a word that has been removed from the language of modernism. I'm surprised you even mention it. It seems as if we forget that there are hidden reasons...

Double Bind

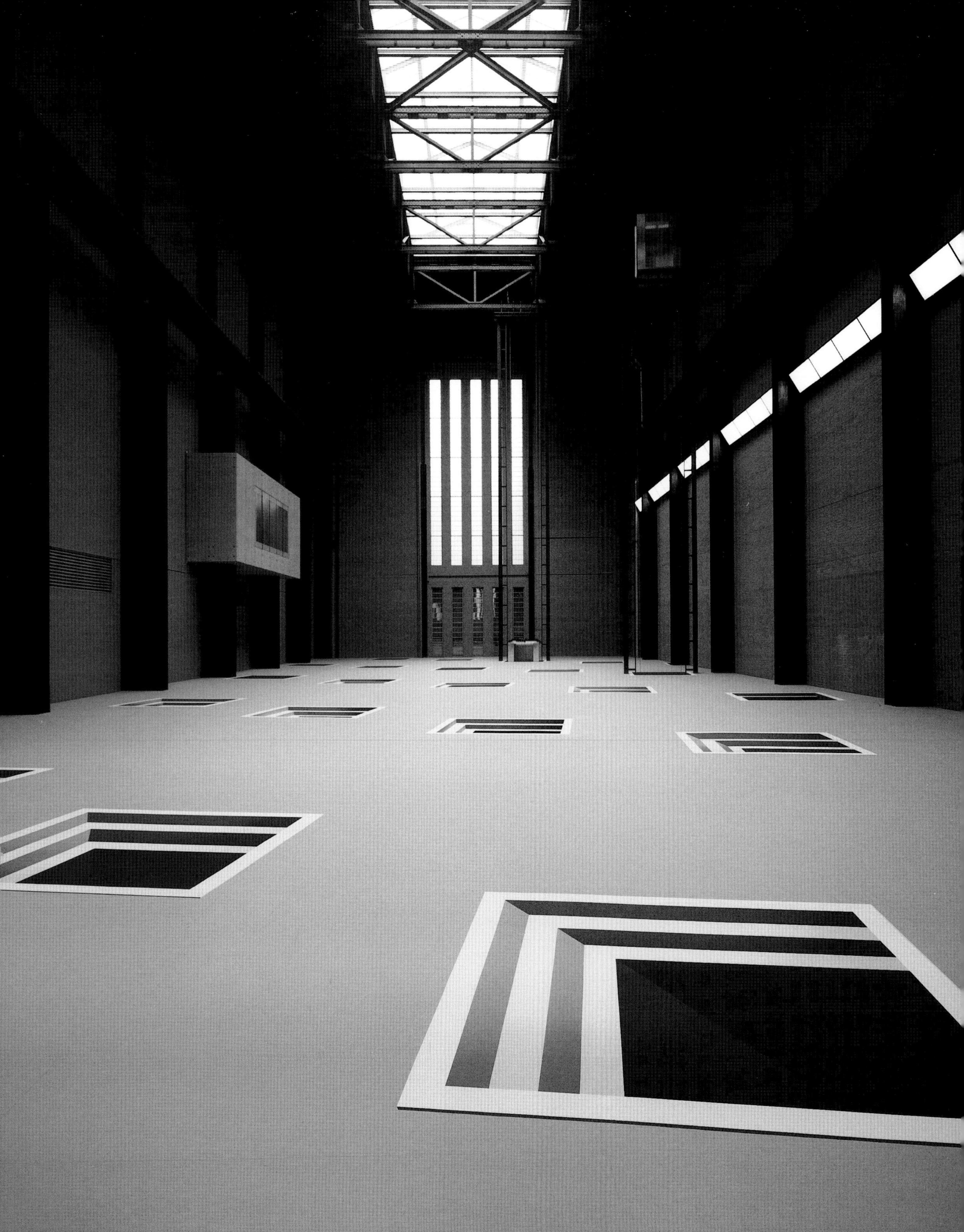

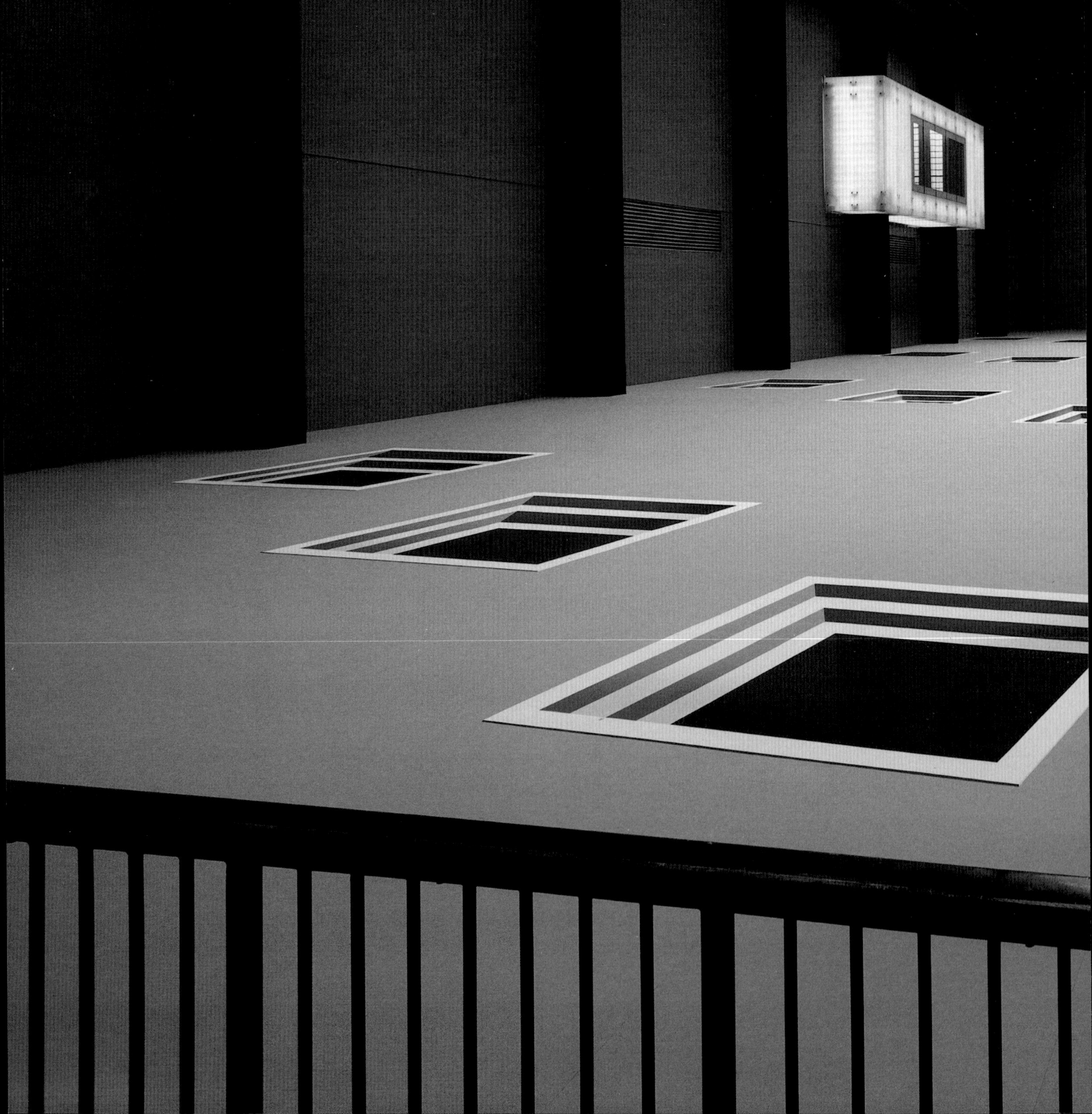

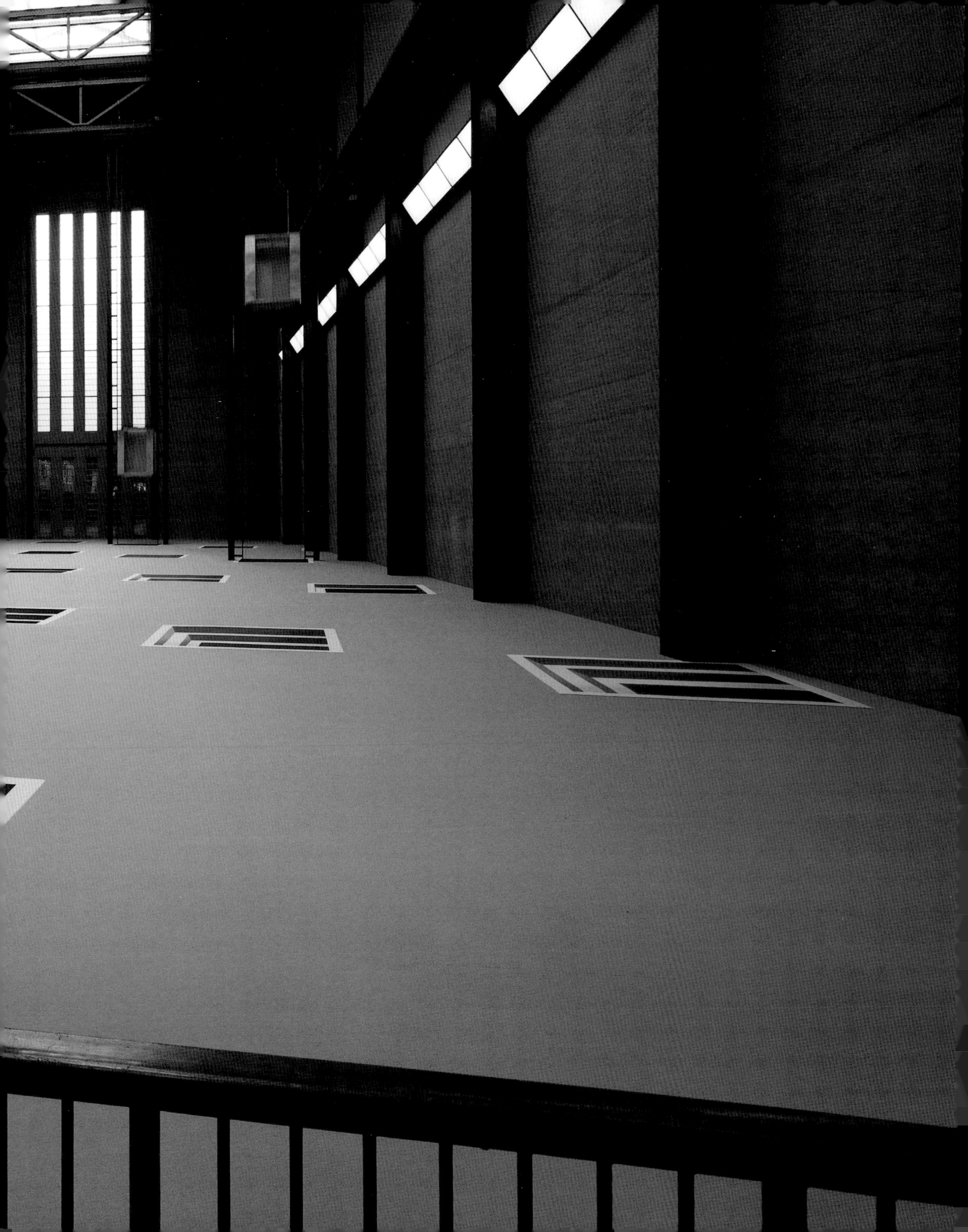

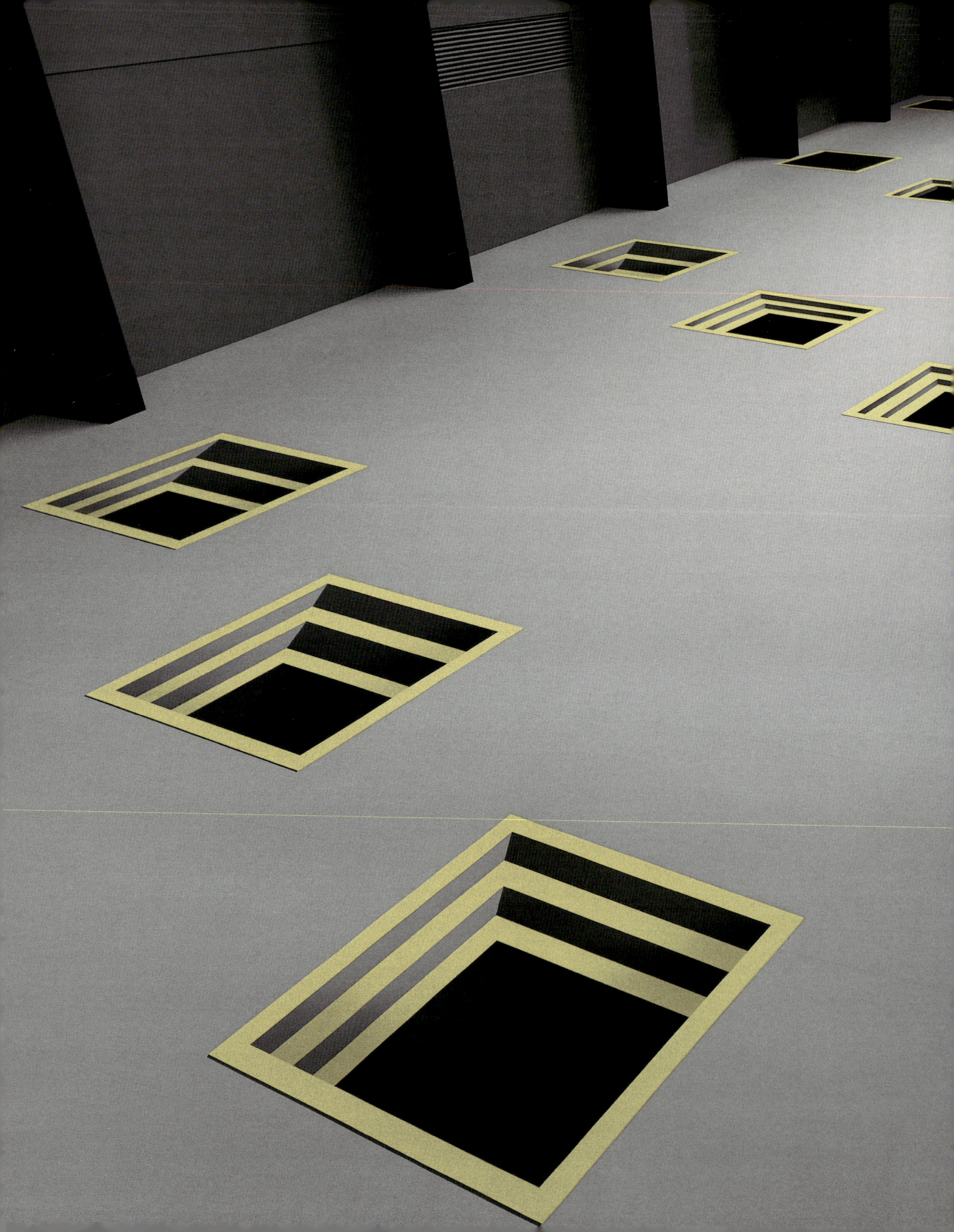

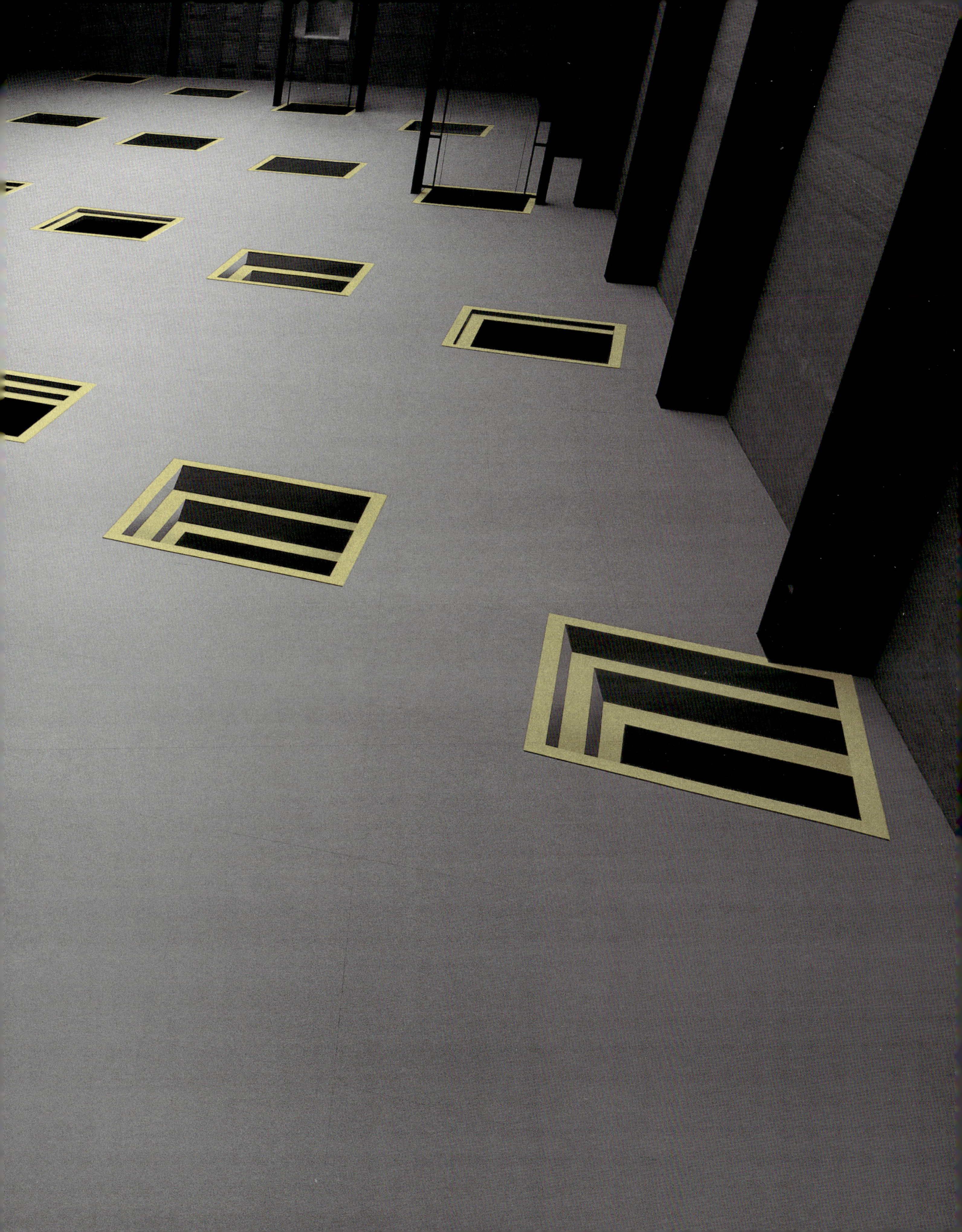

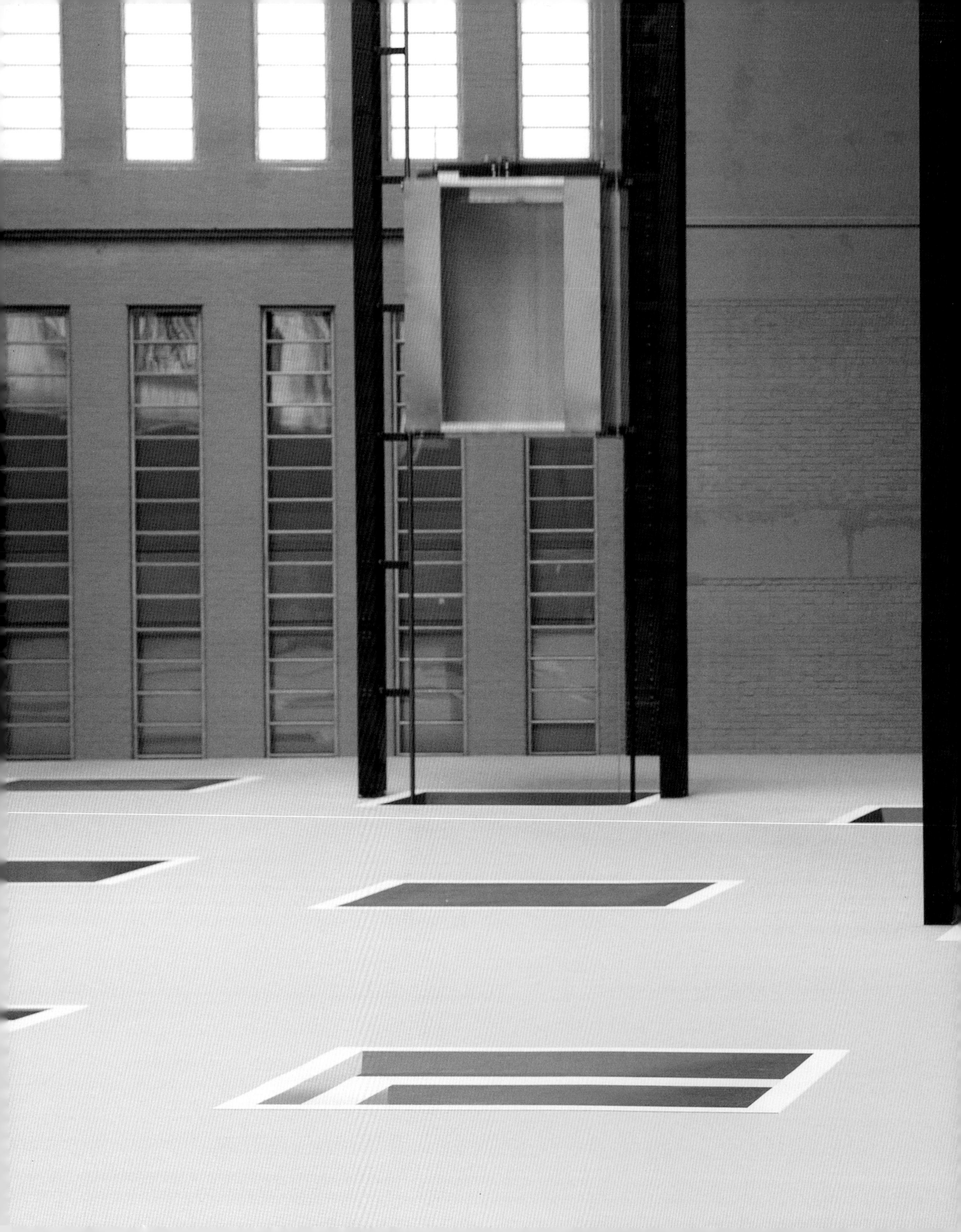

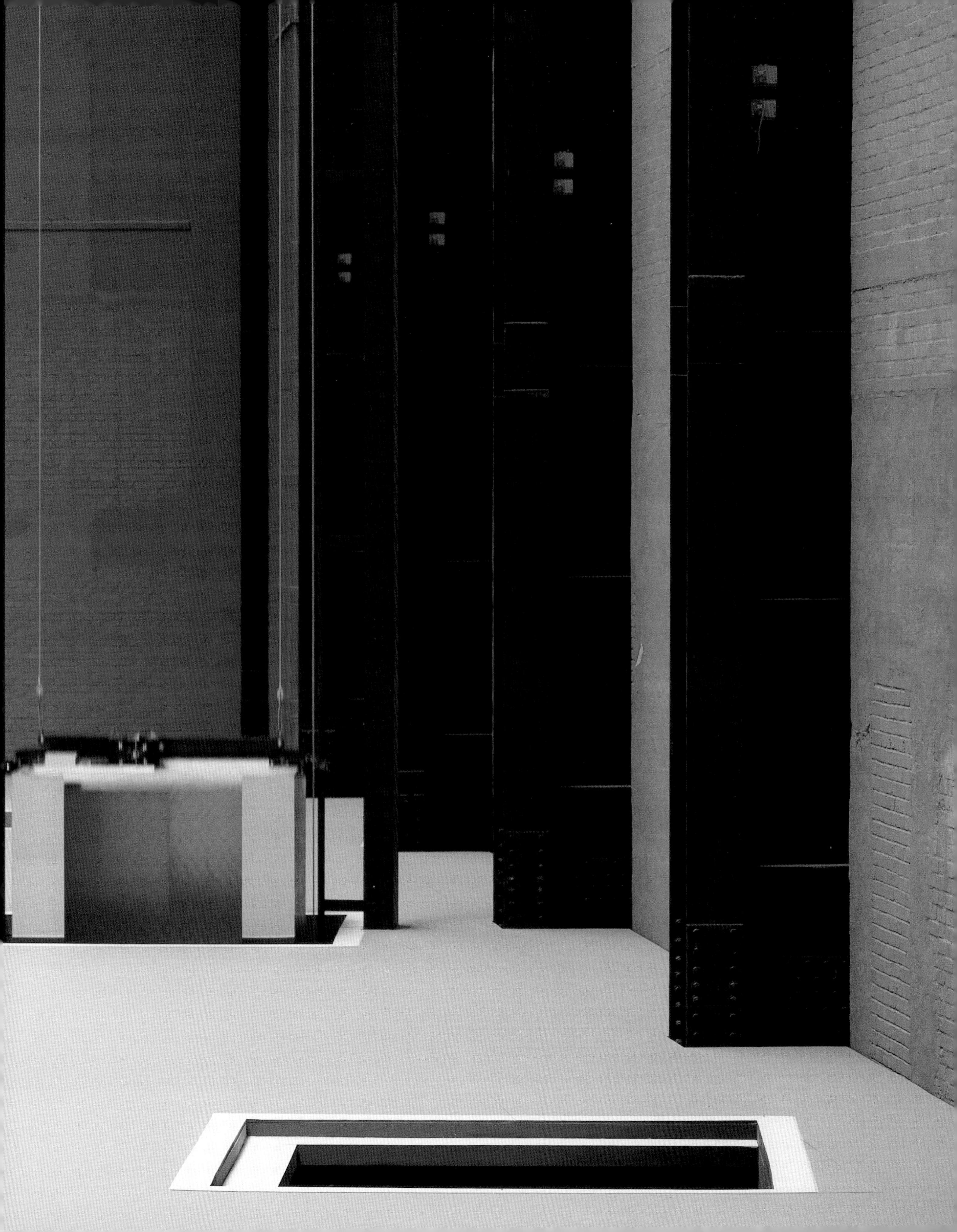

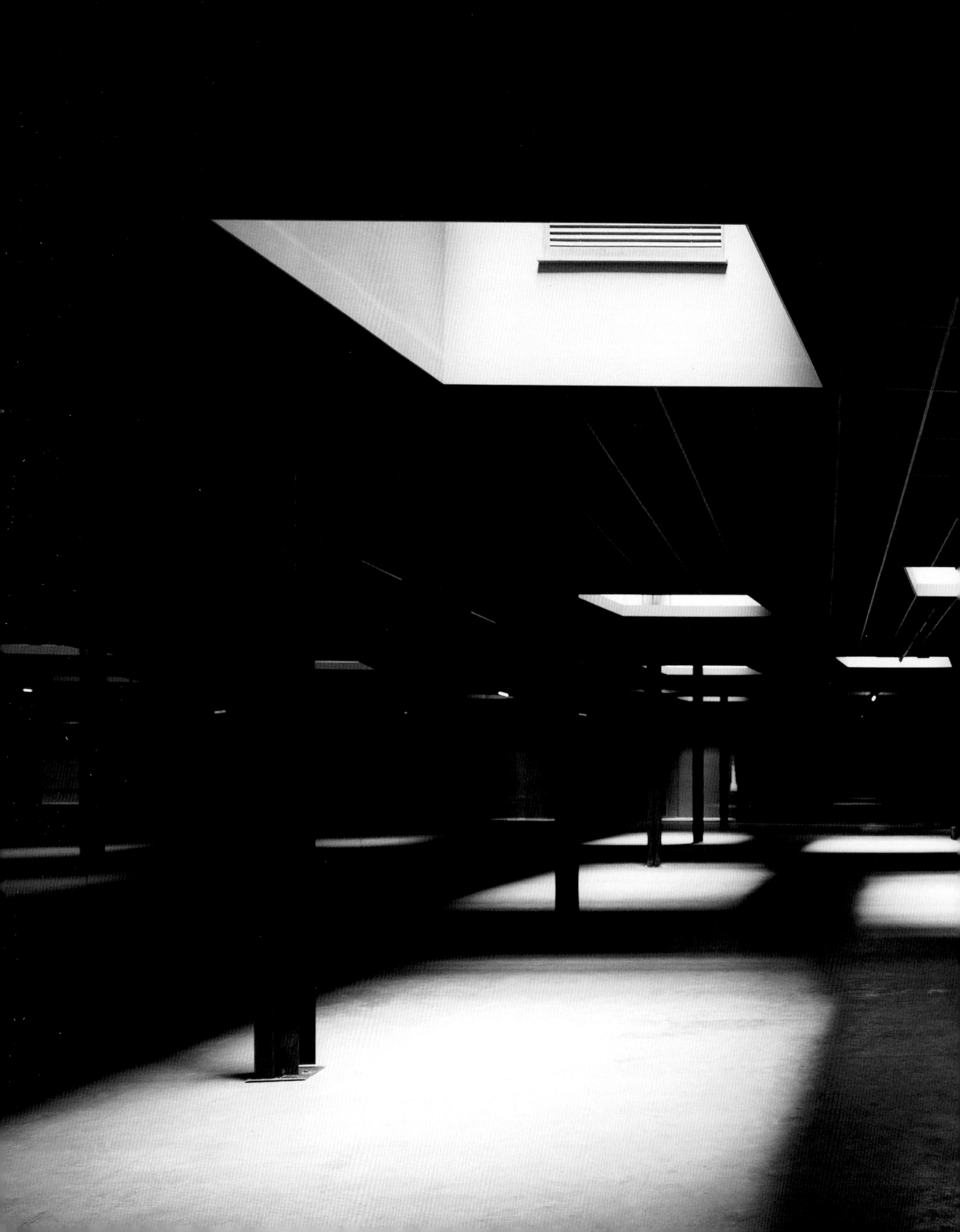

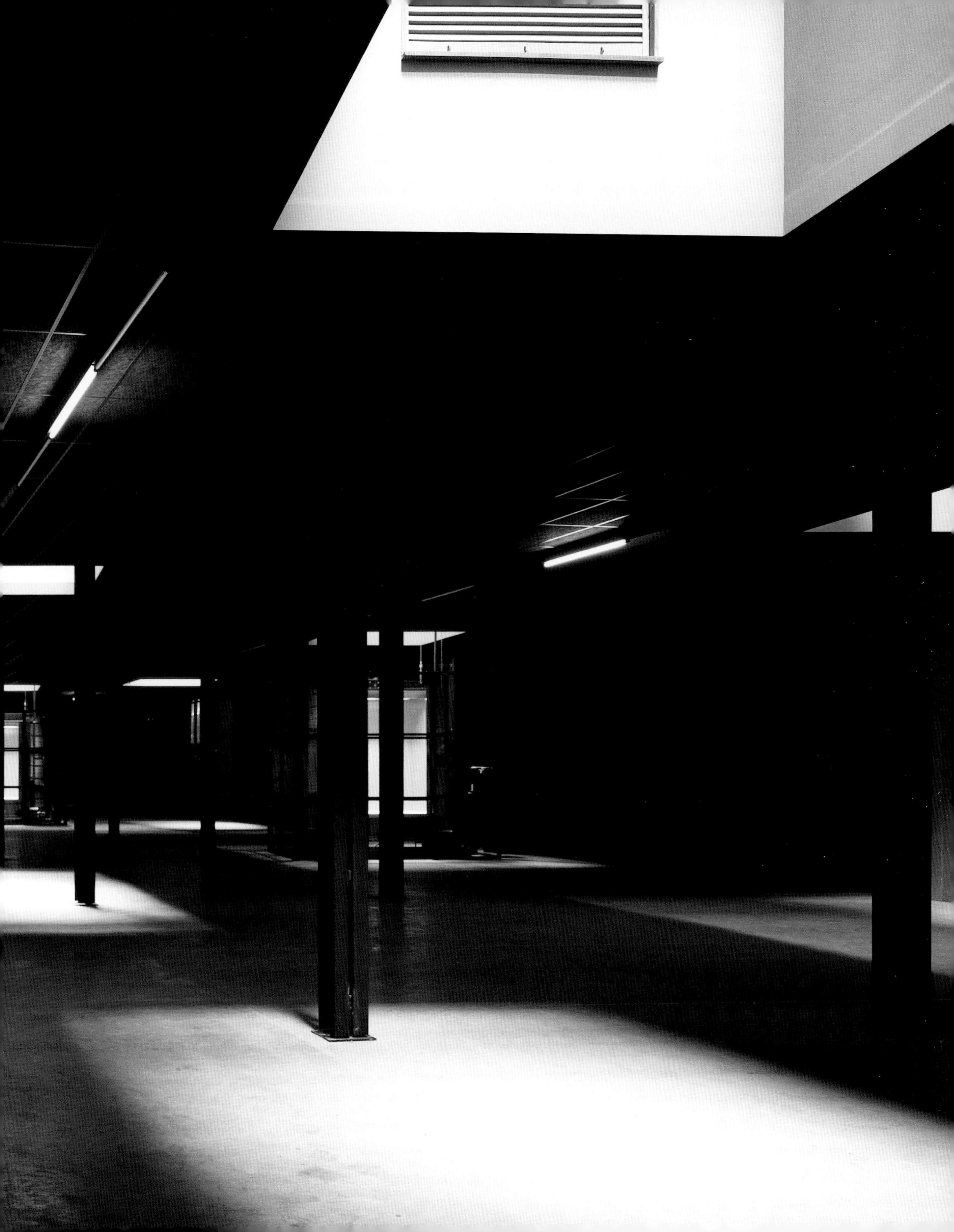

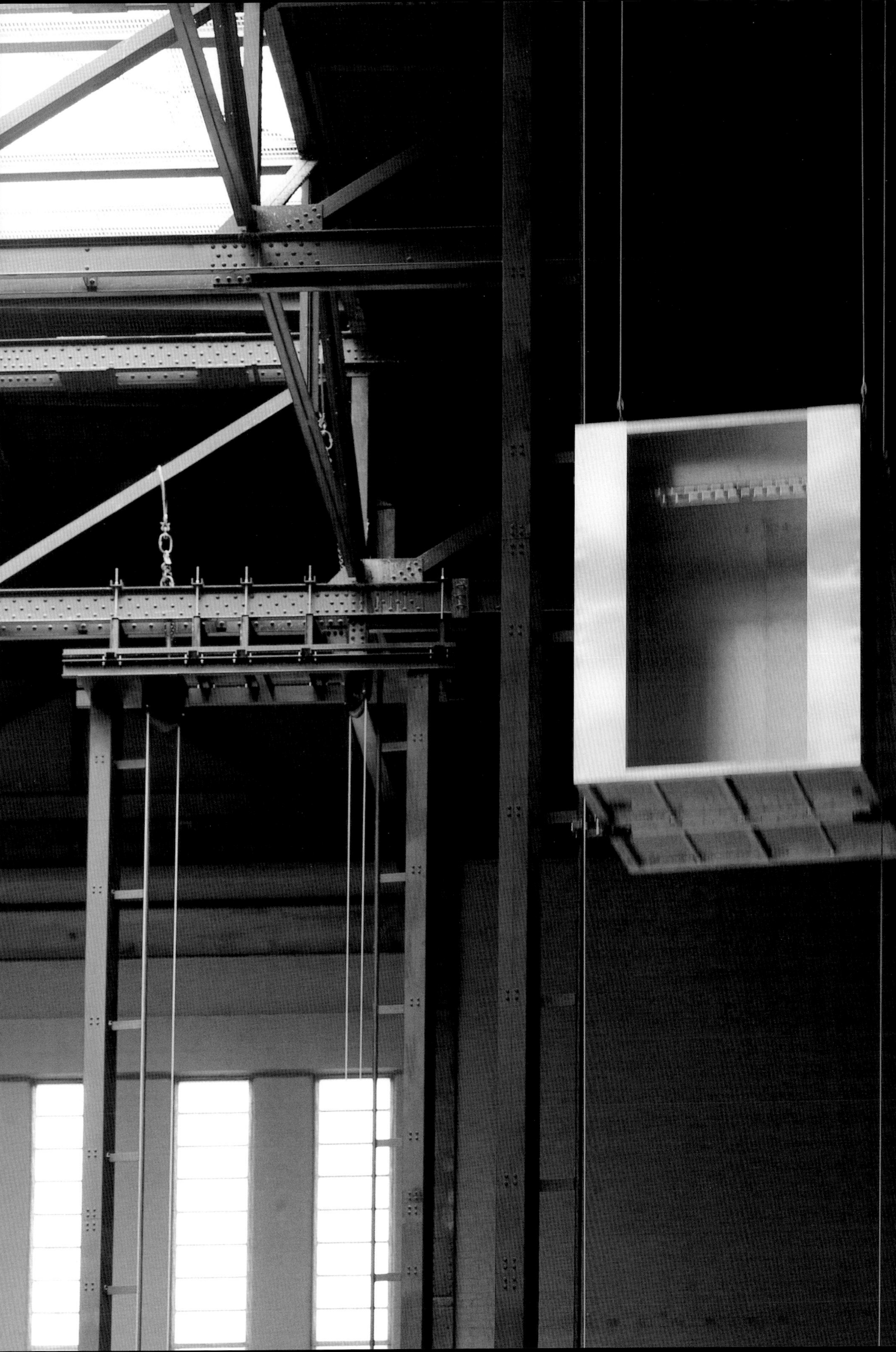

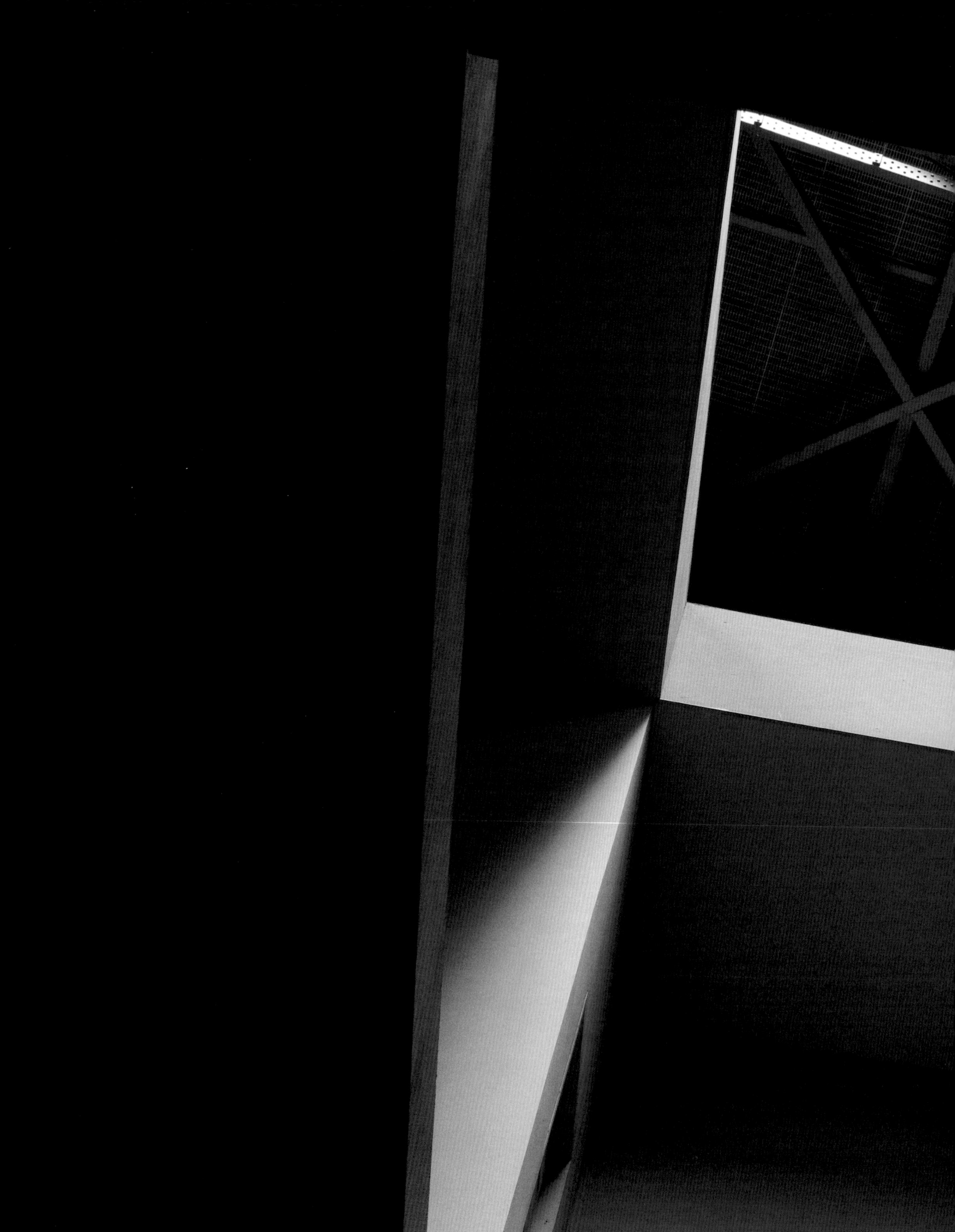

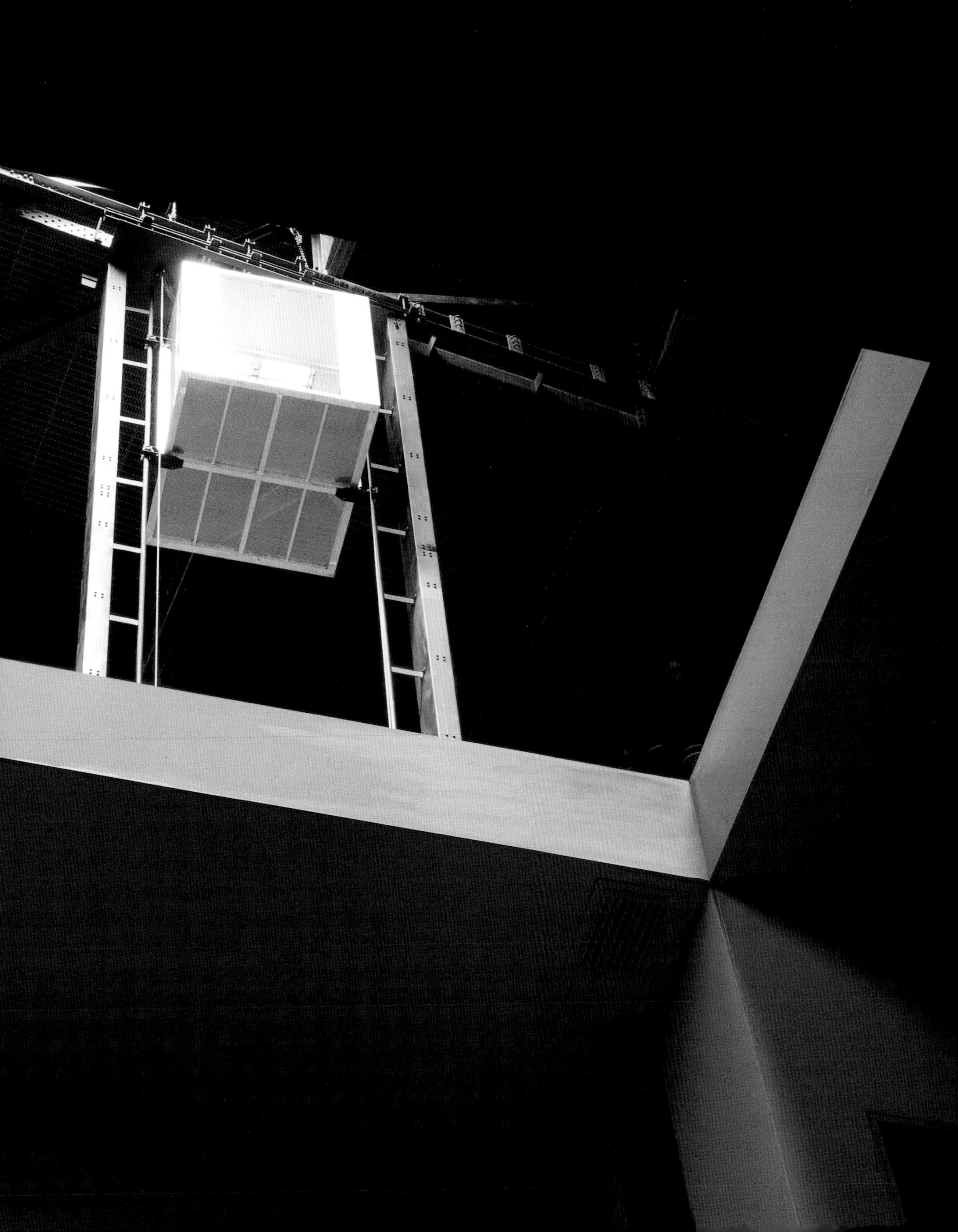

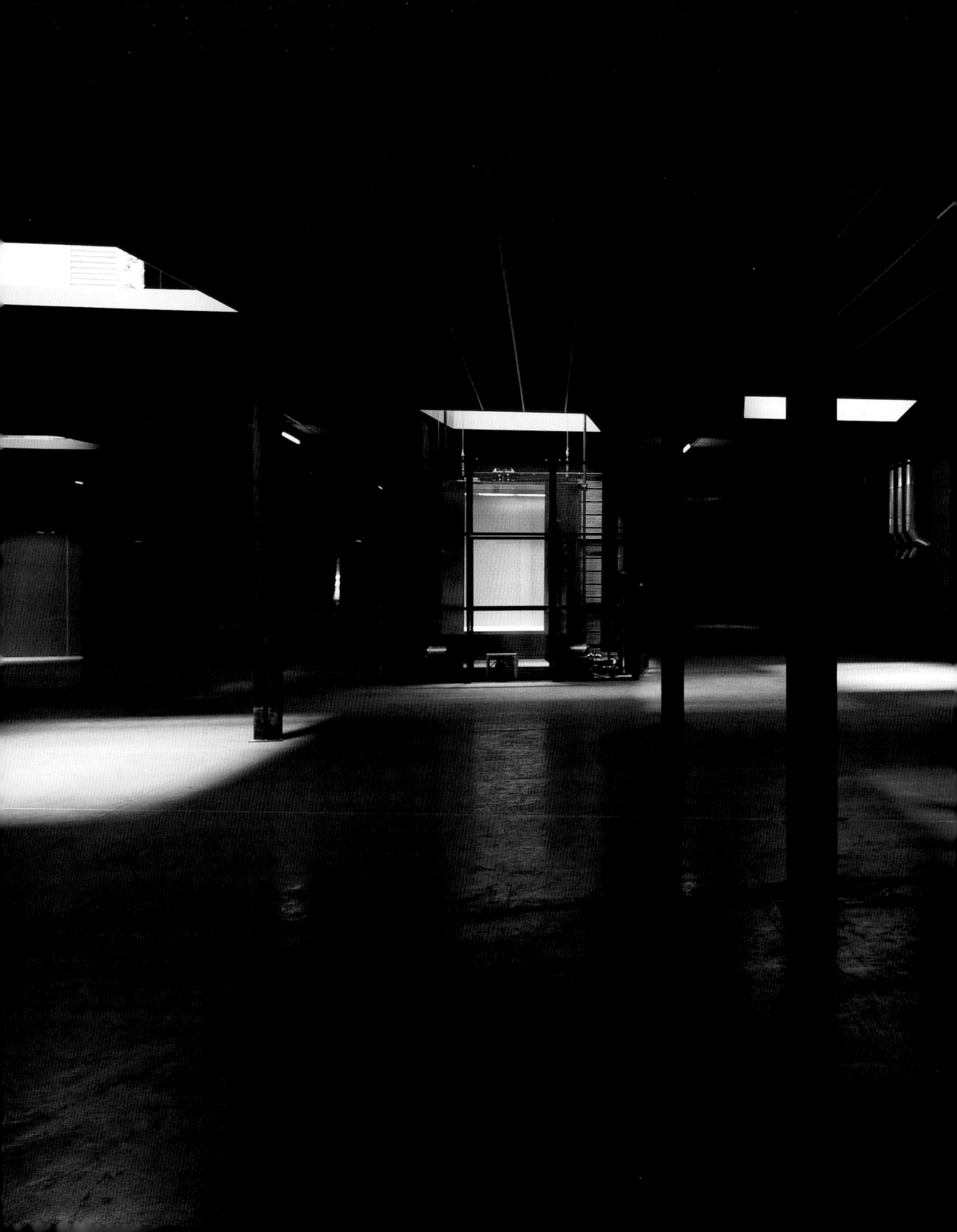

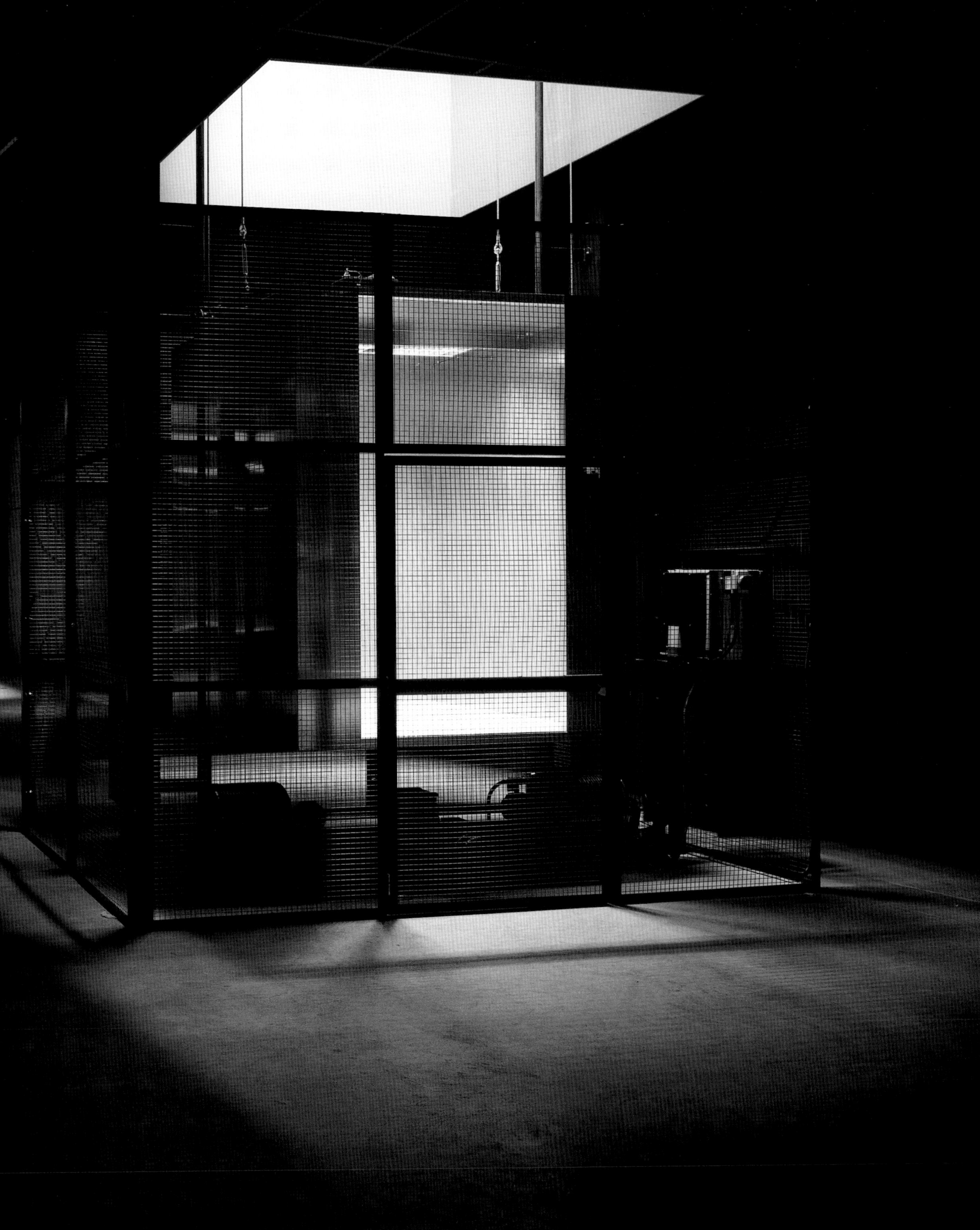

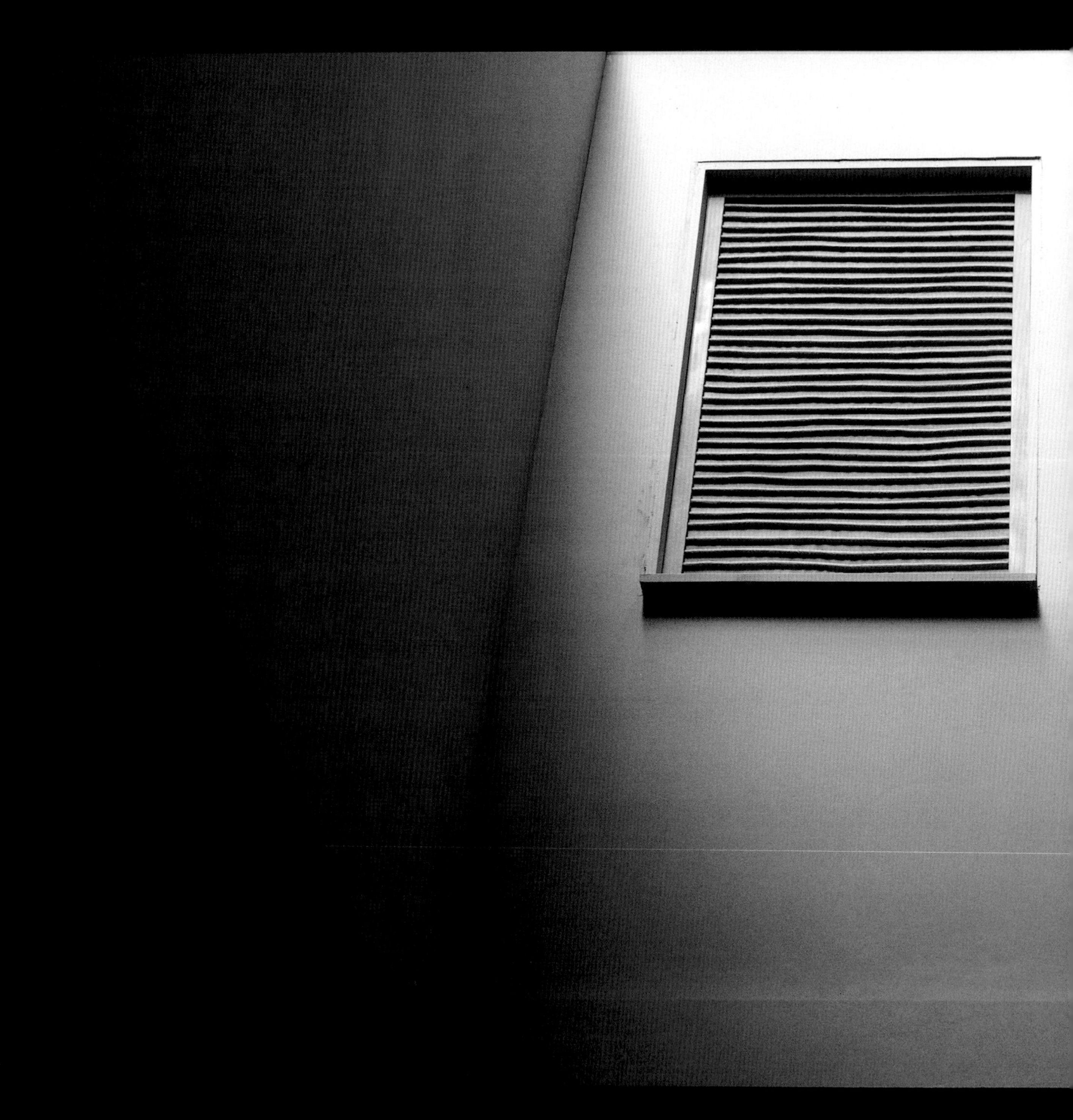

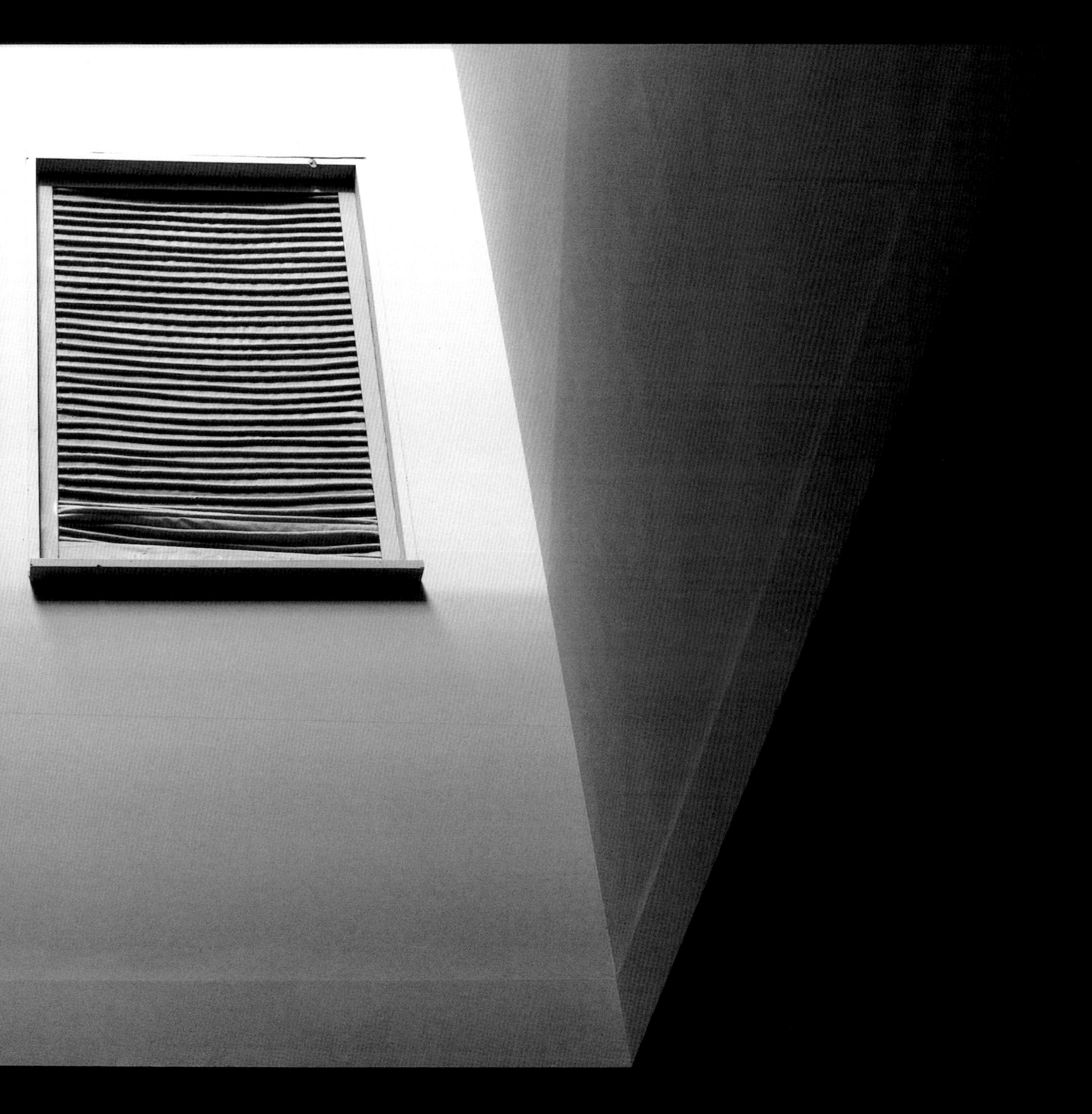

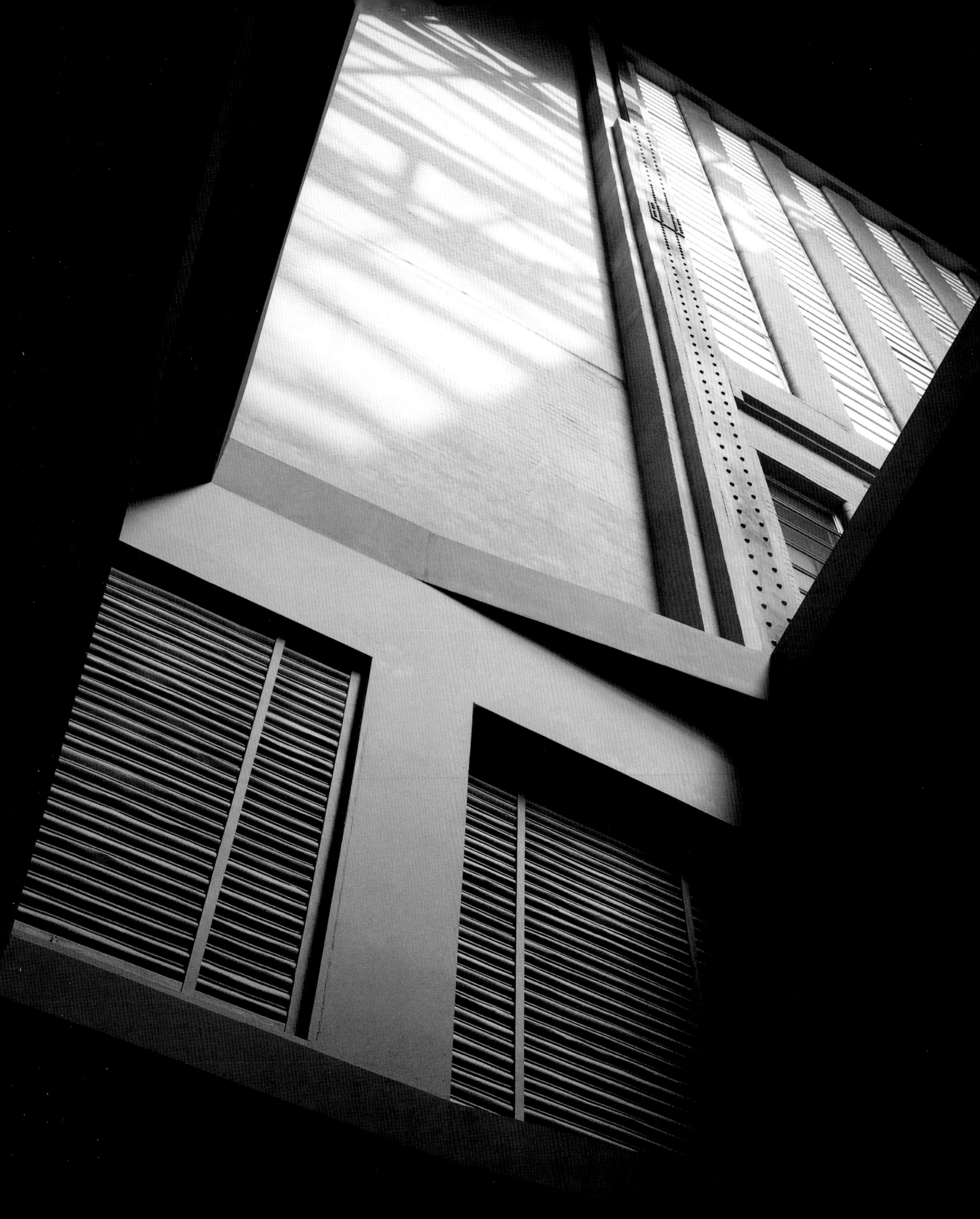

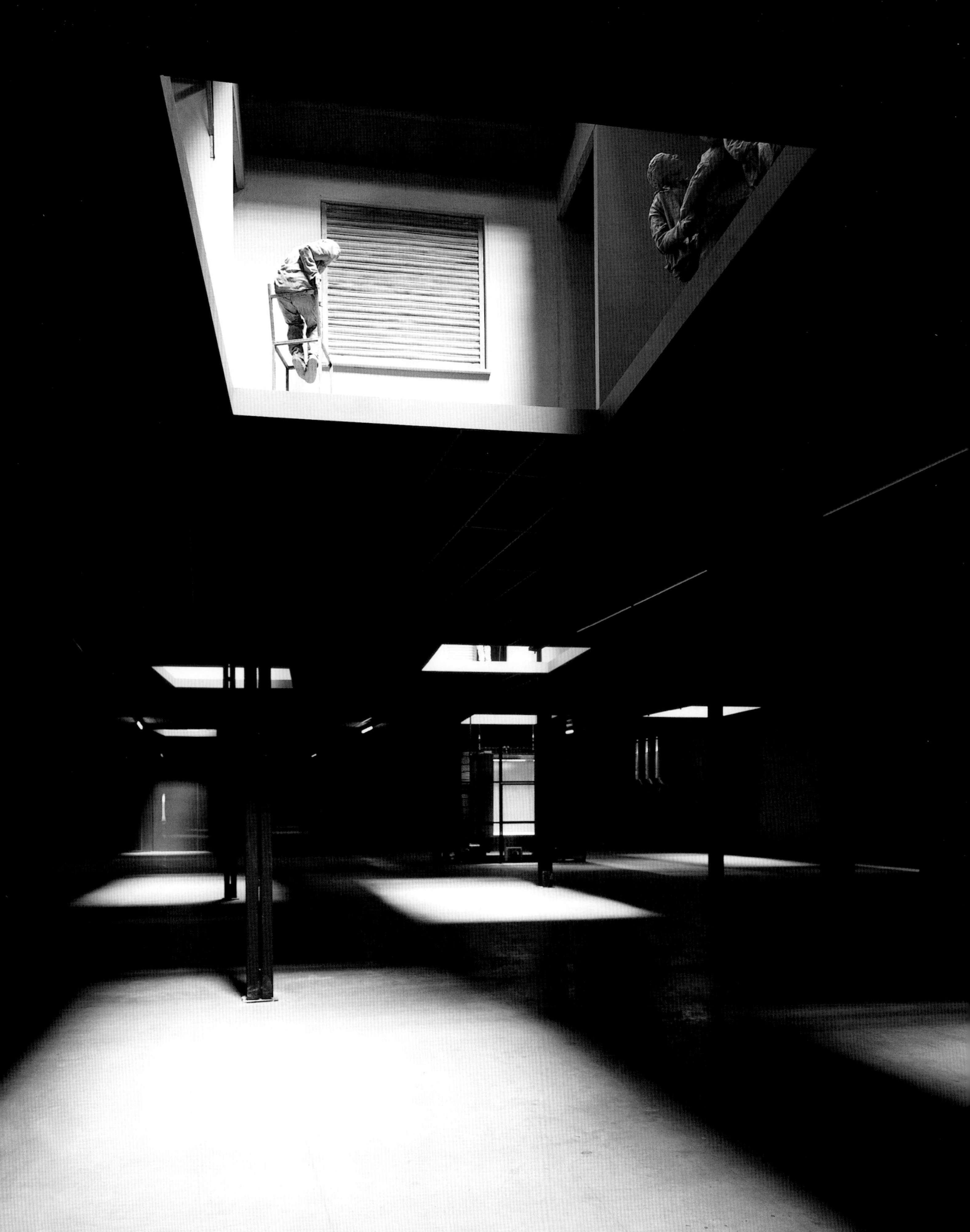

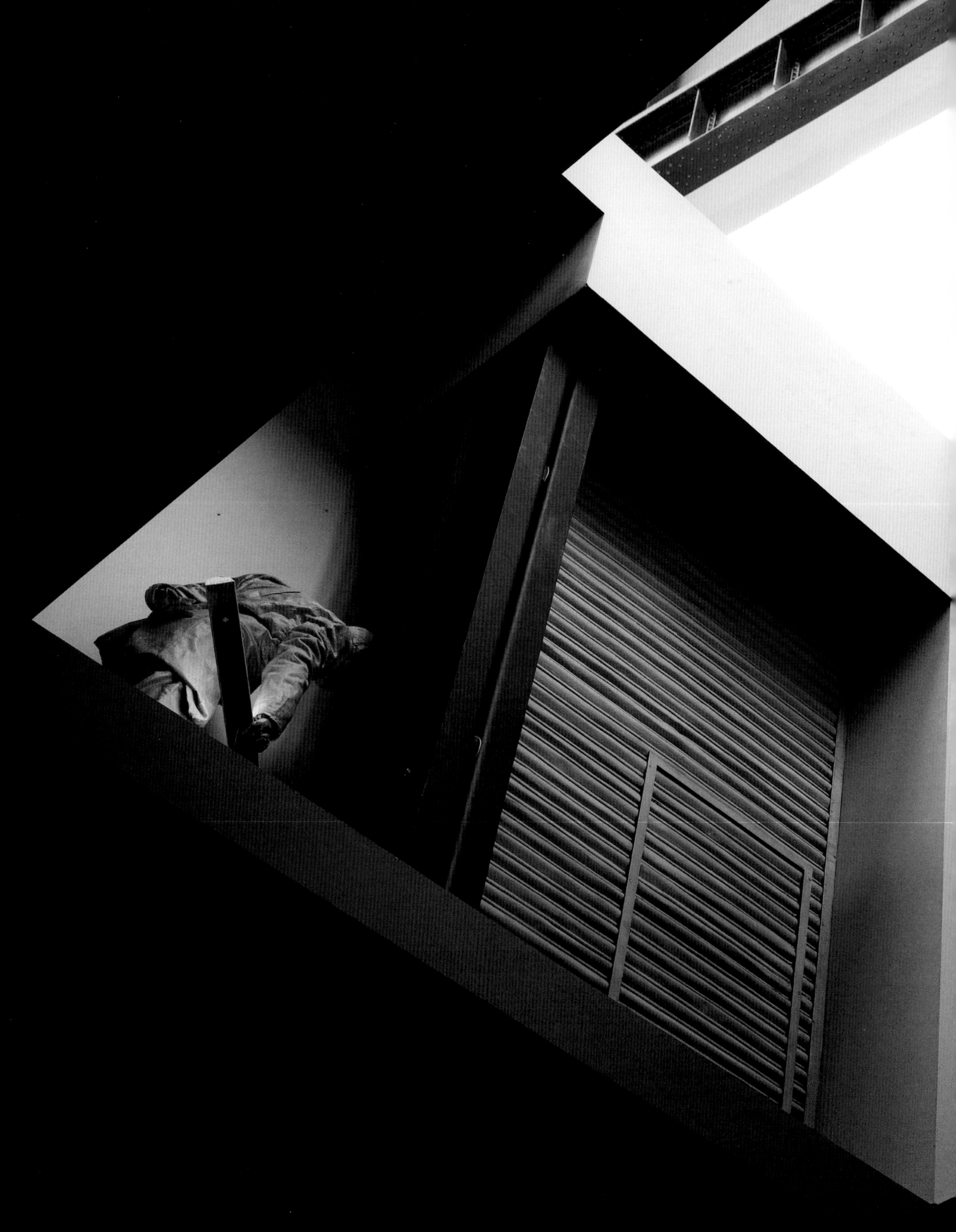

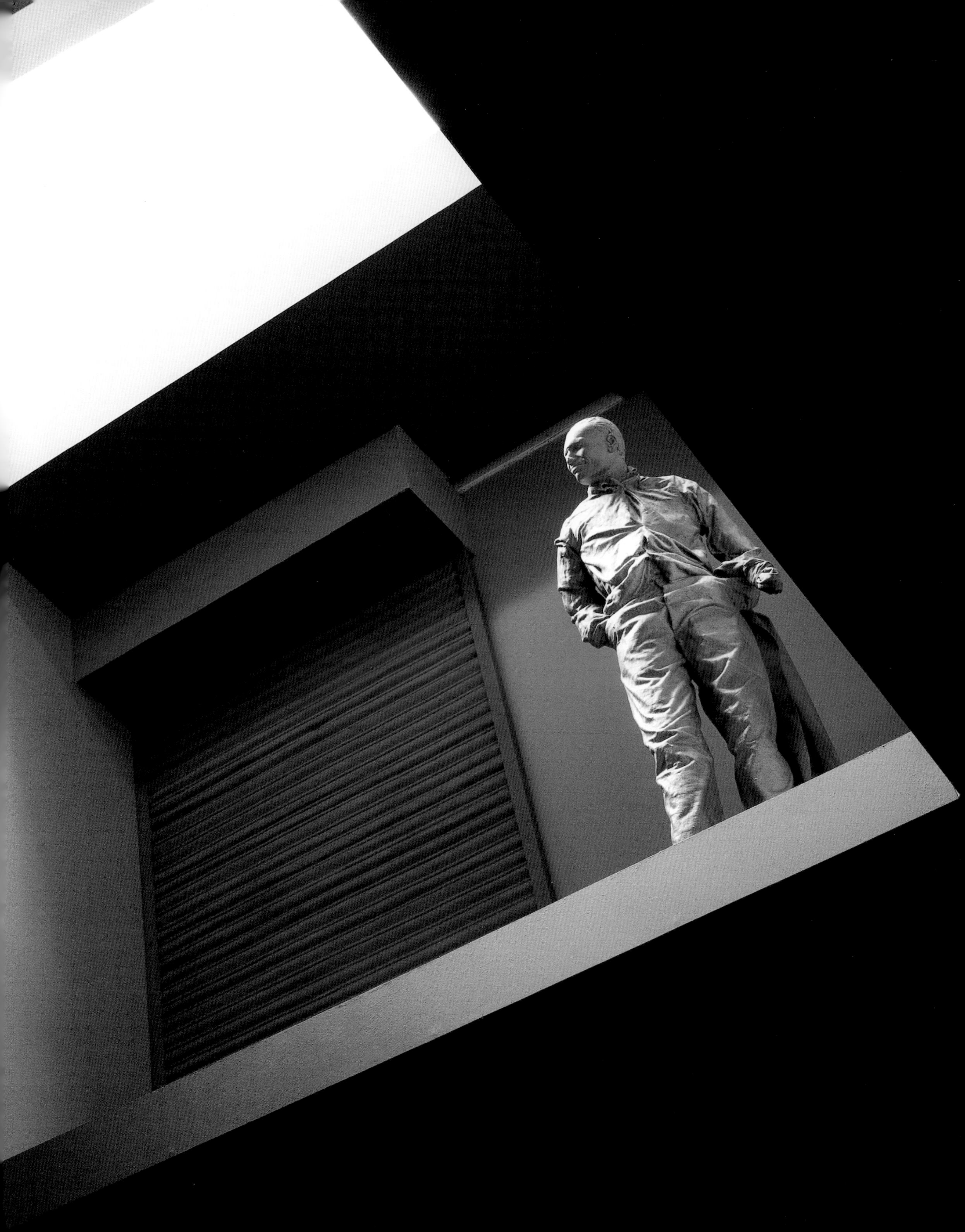

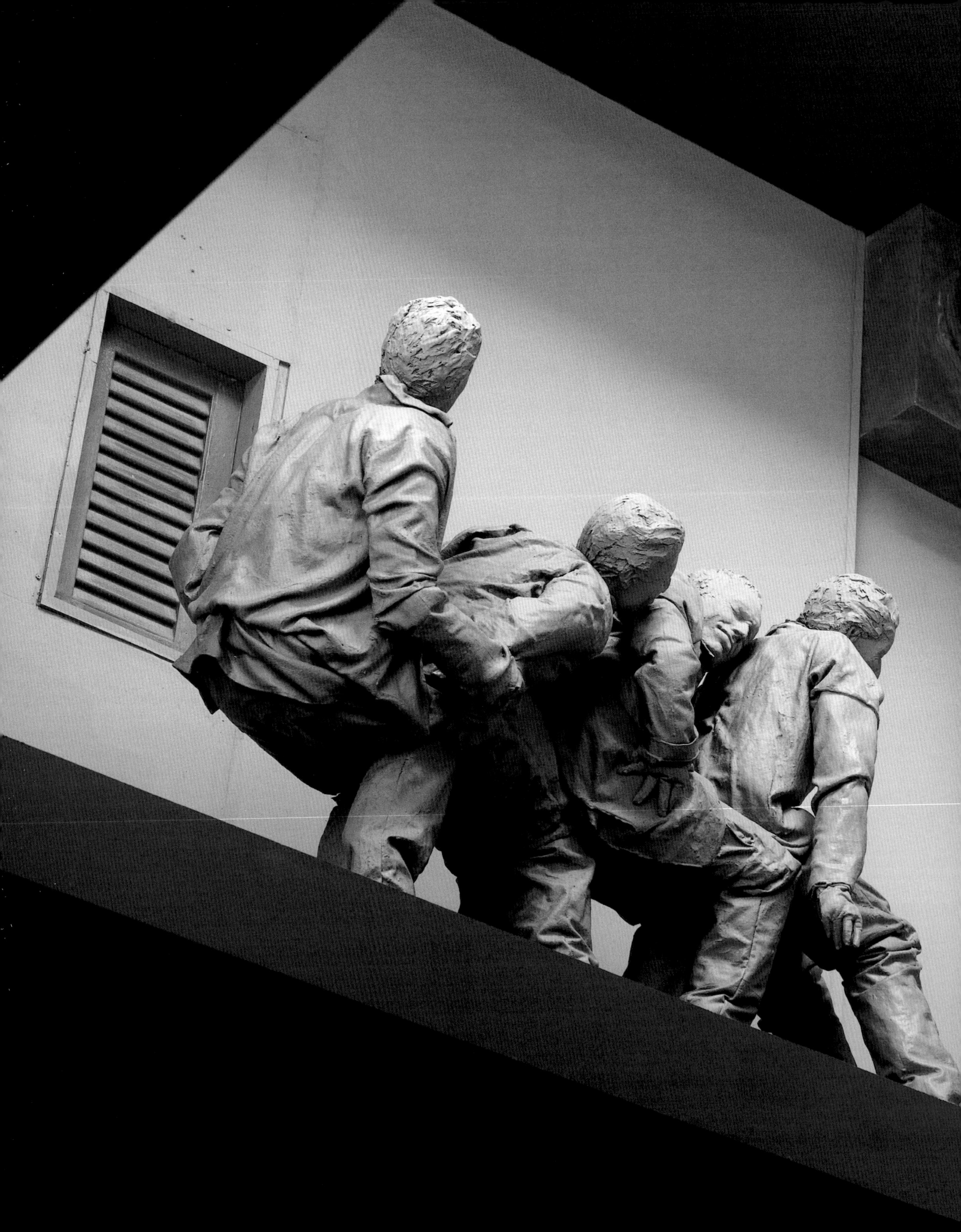

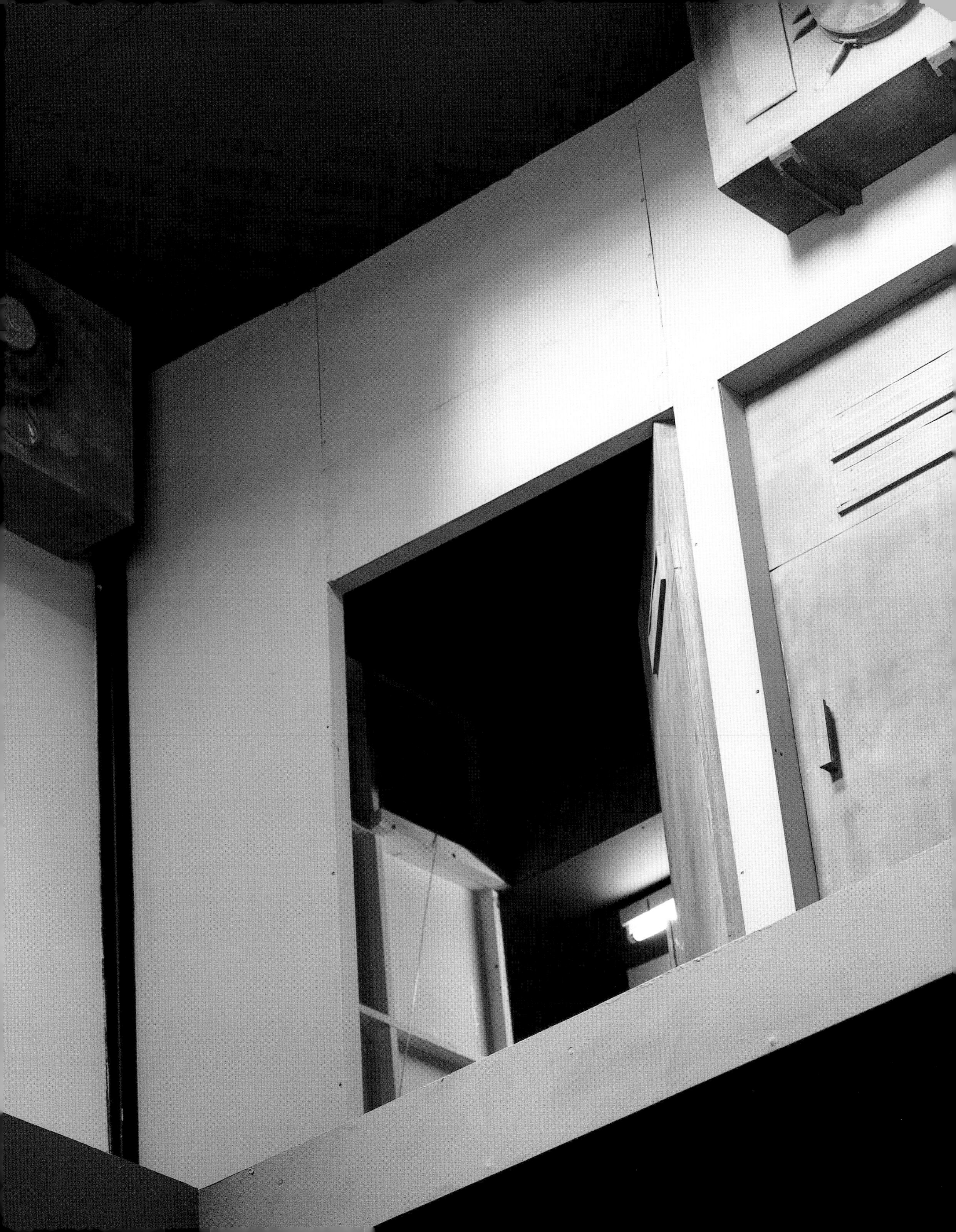

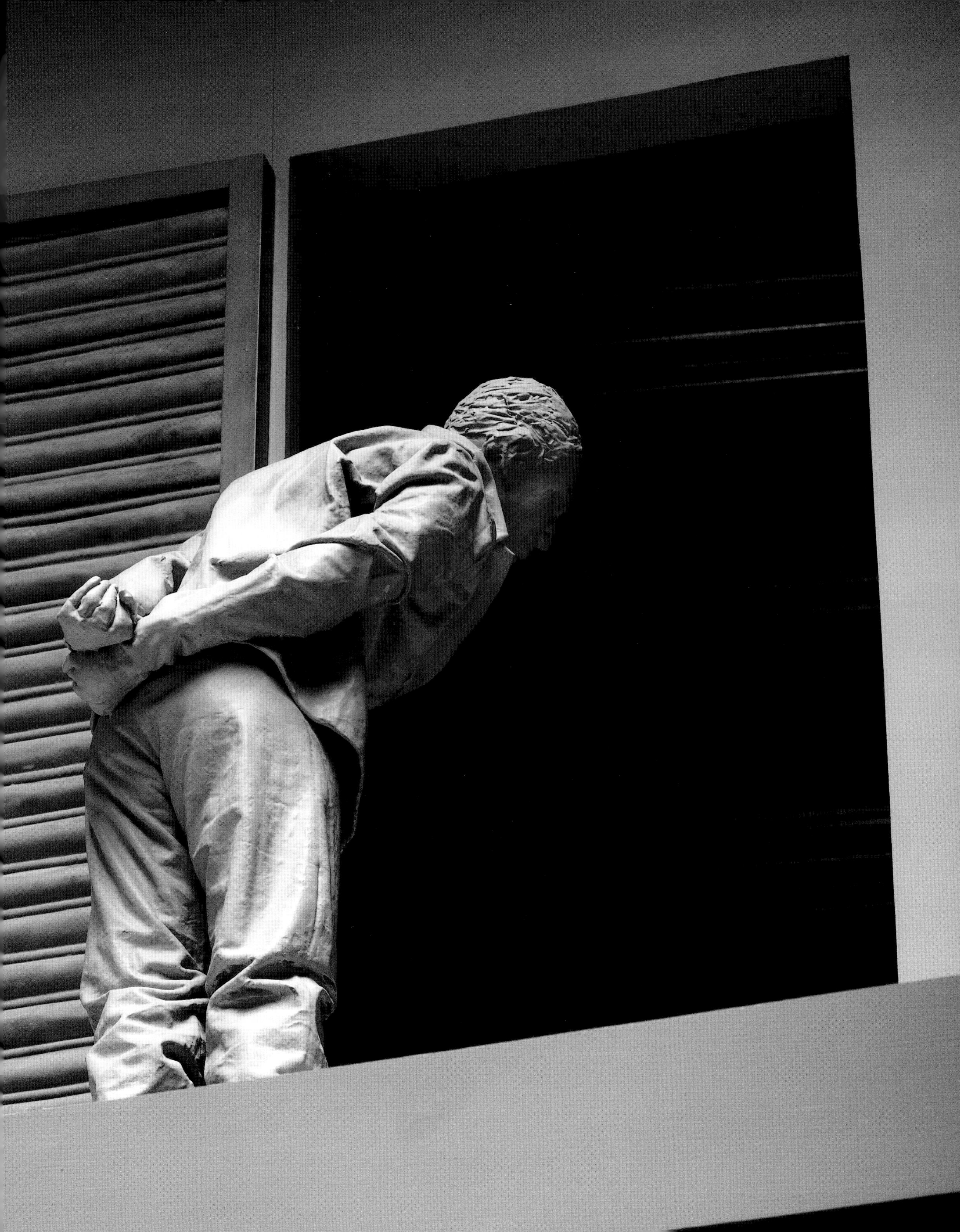

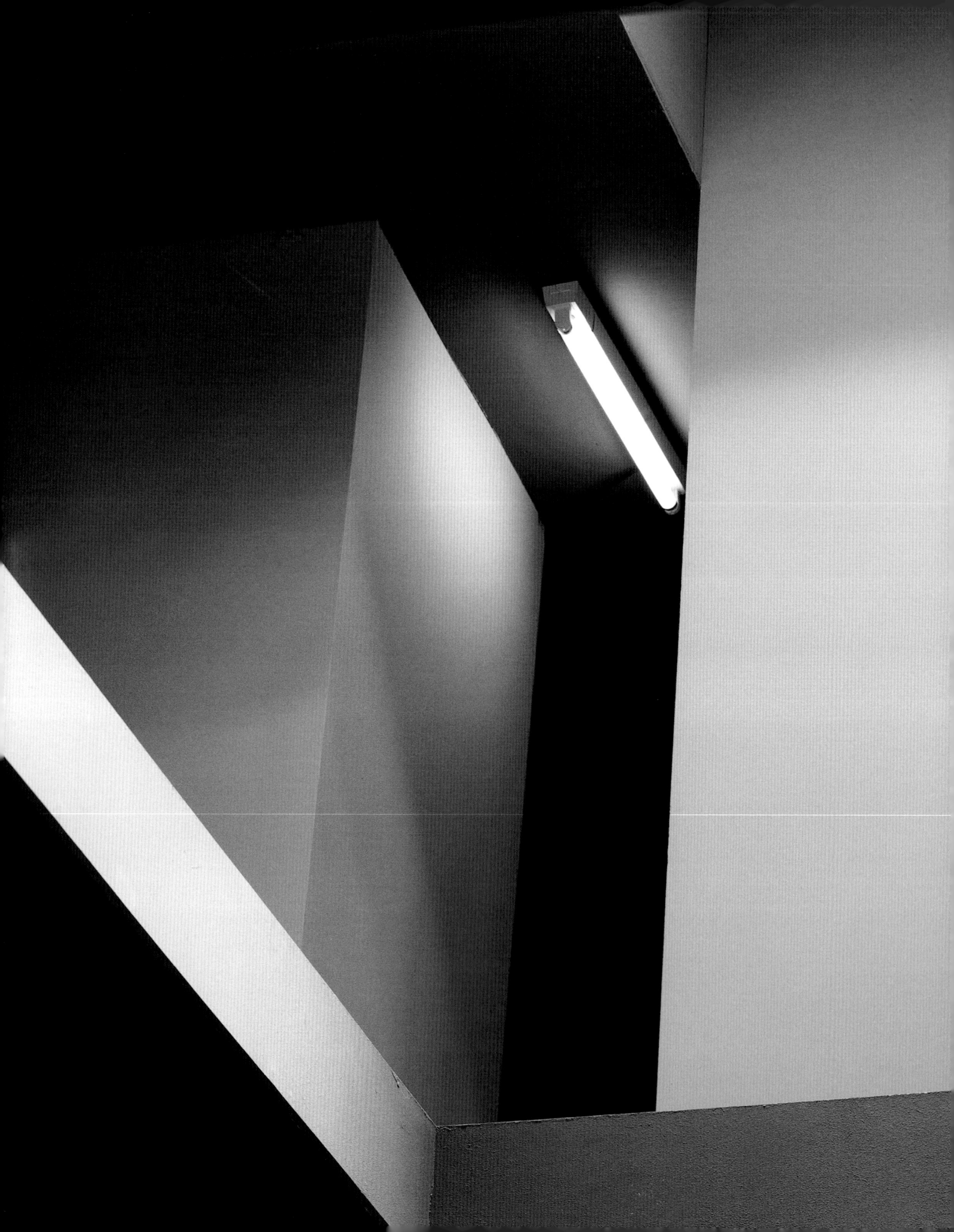

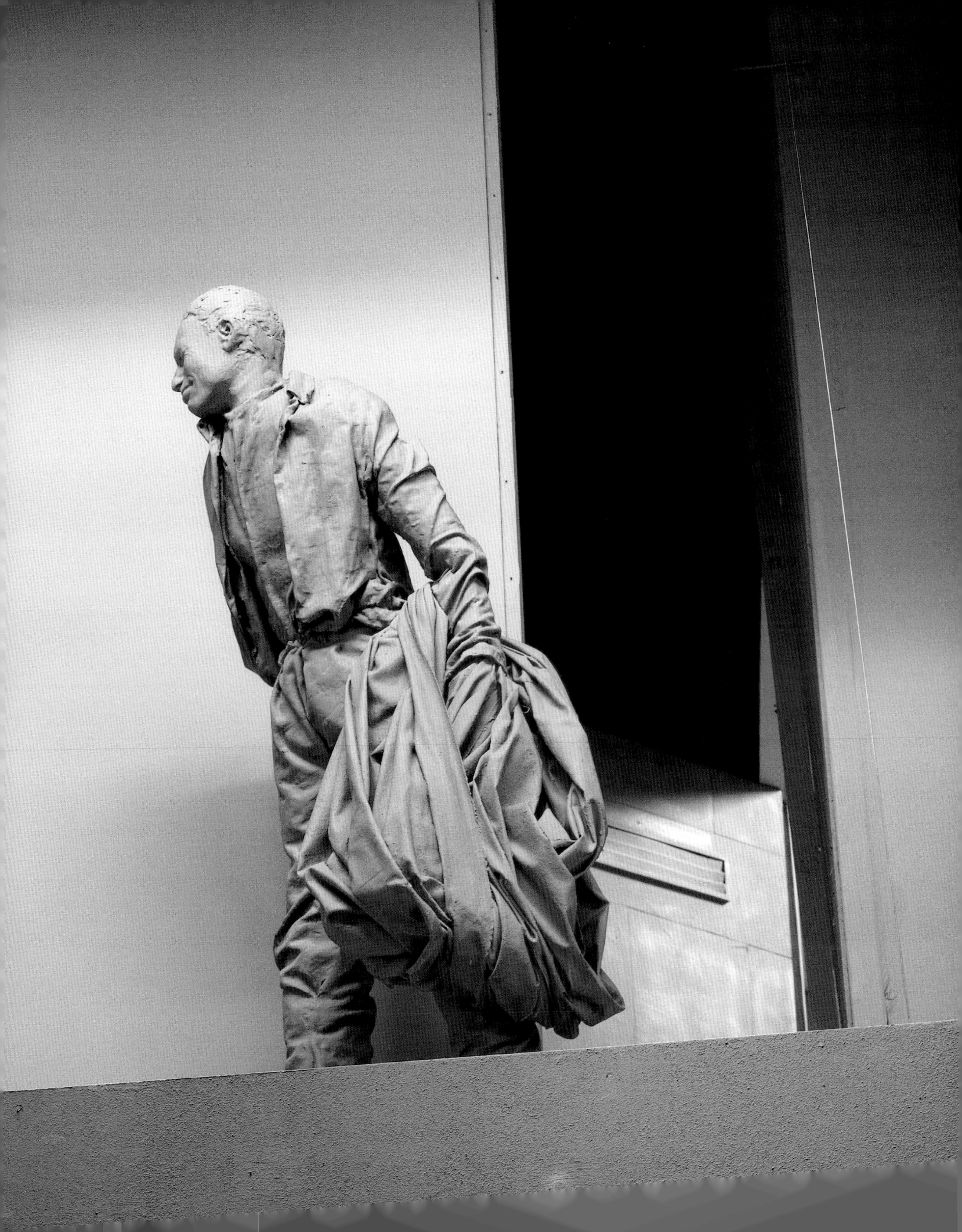

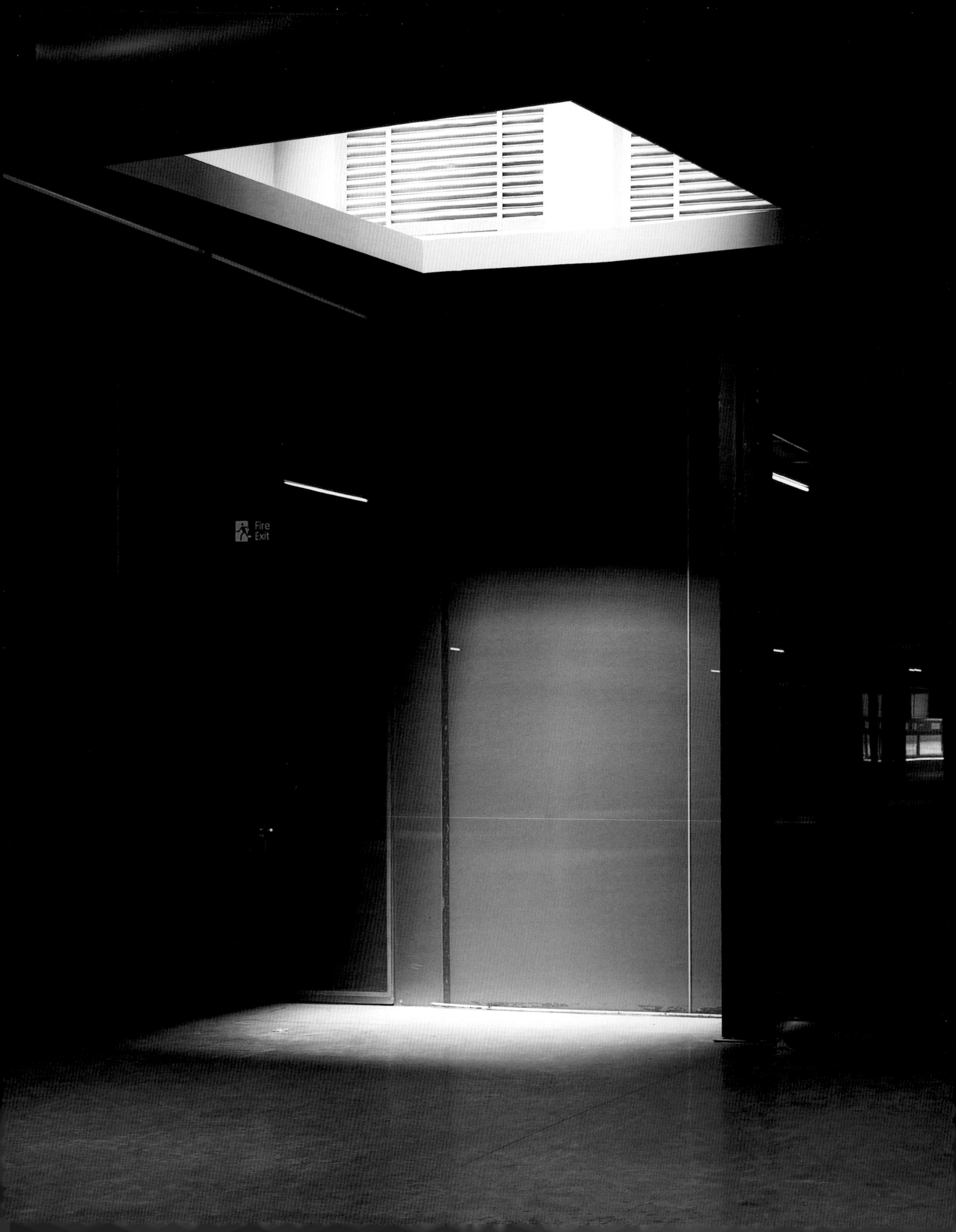

Fire
Exit

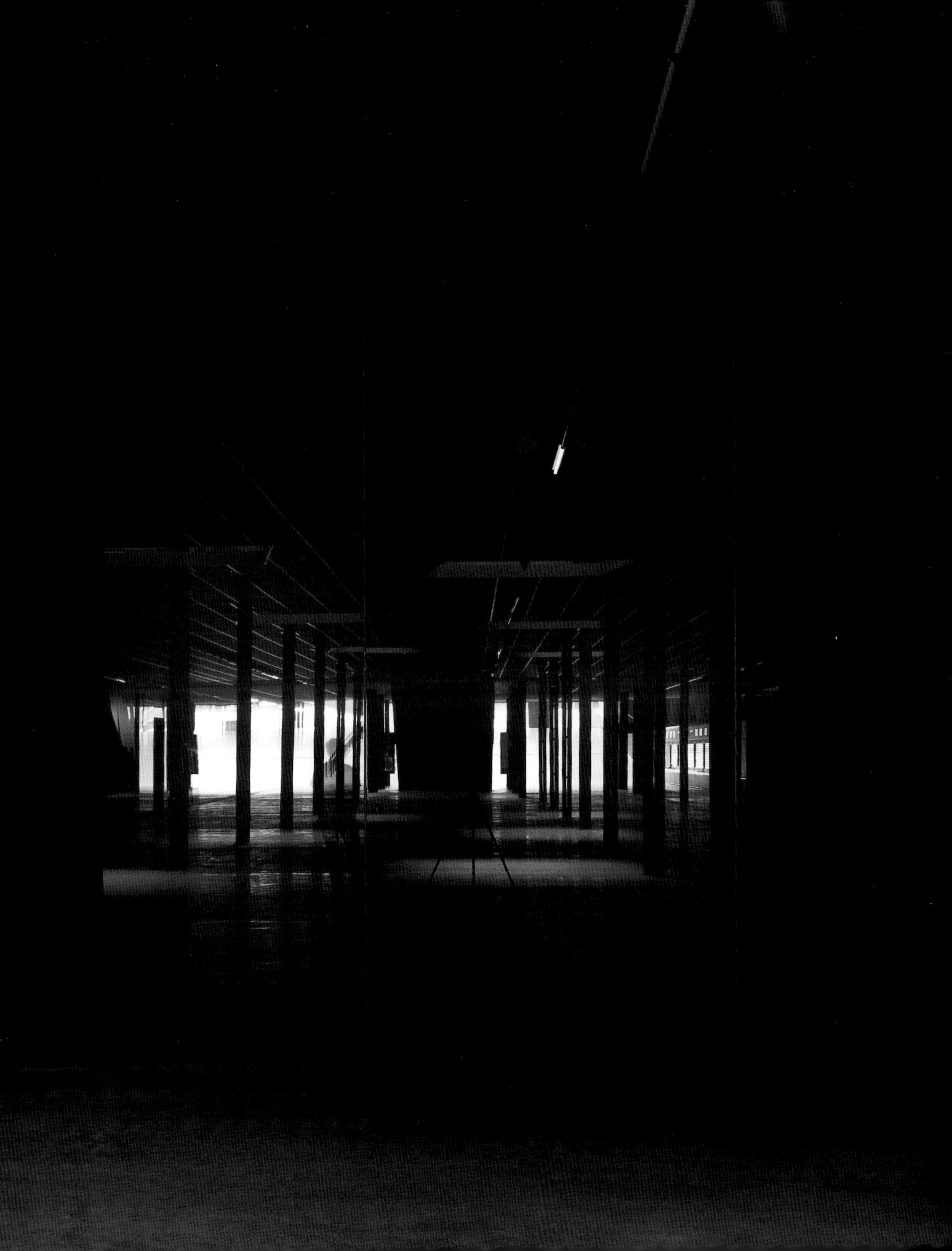

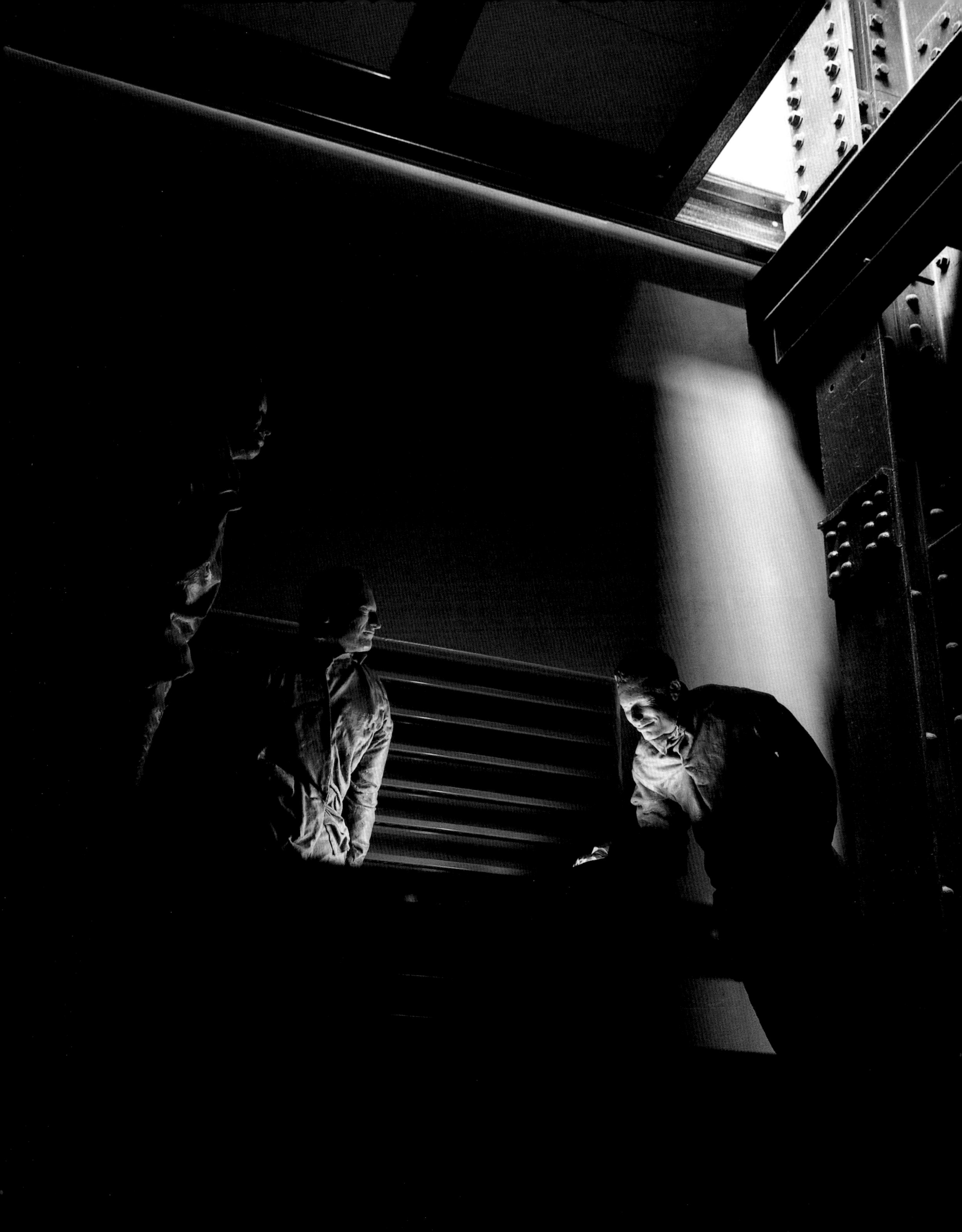

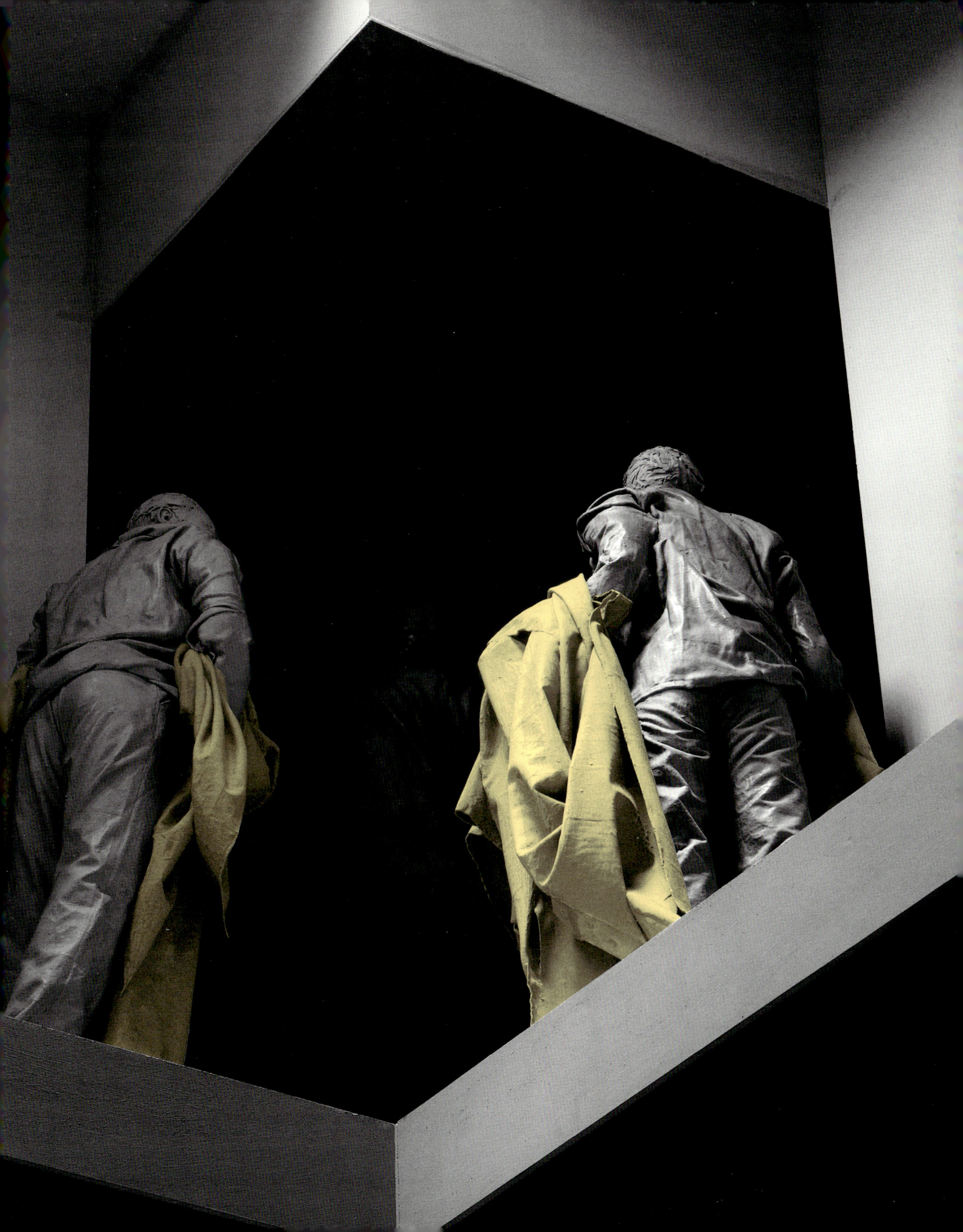

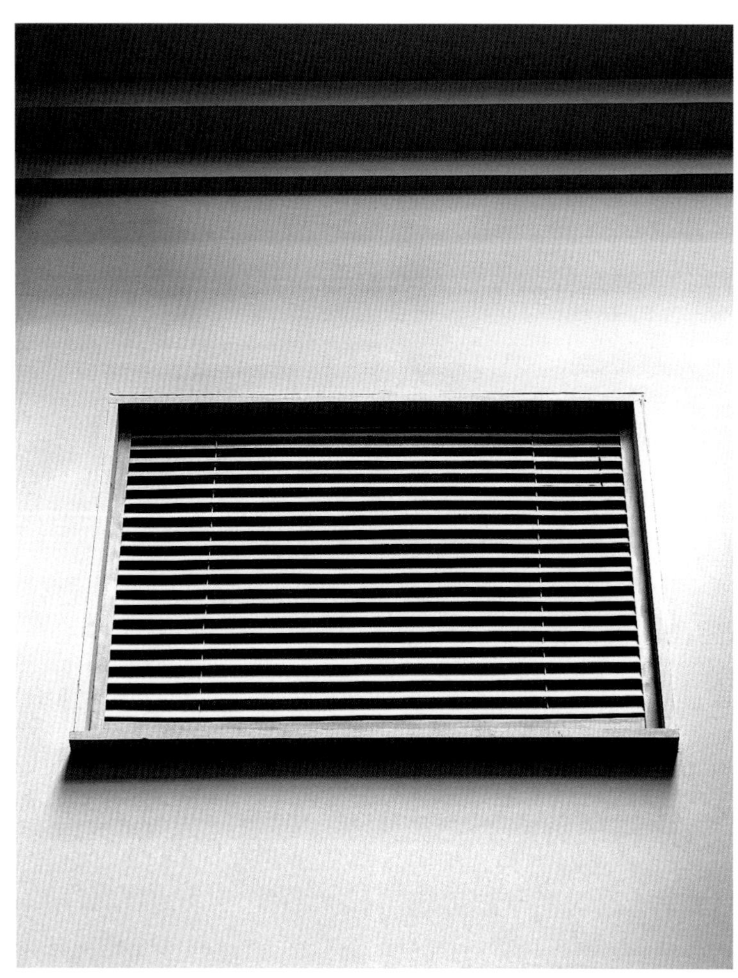

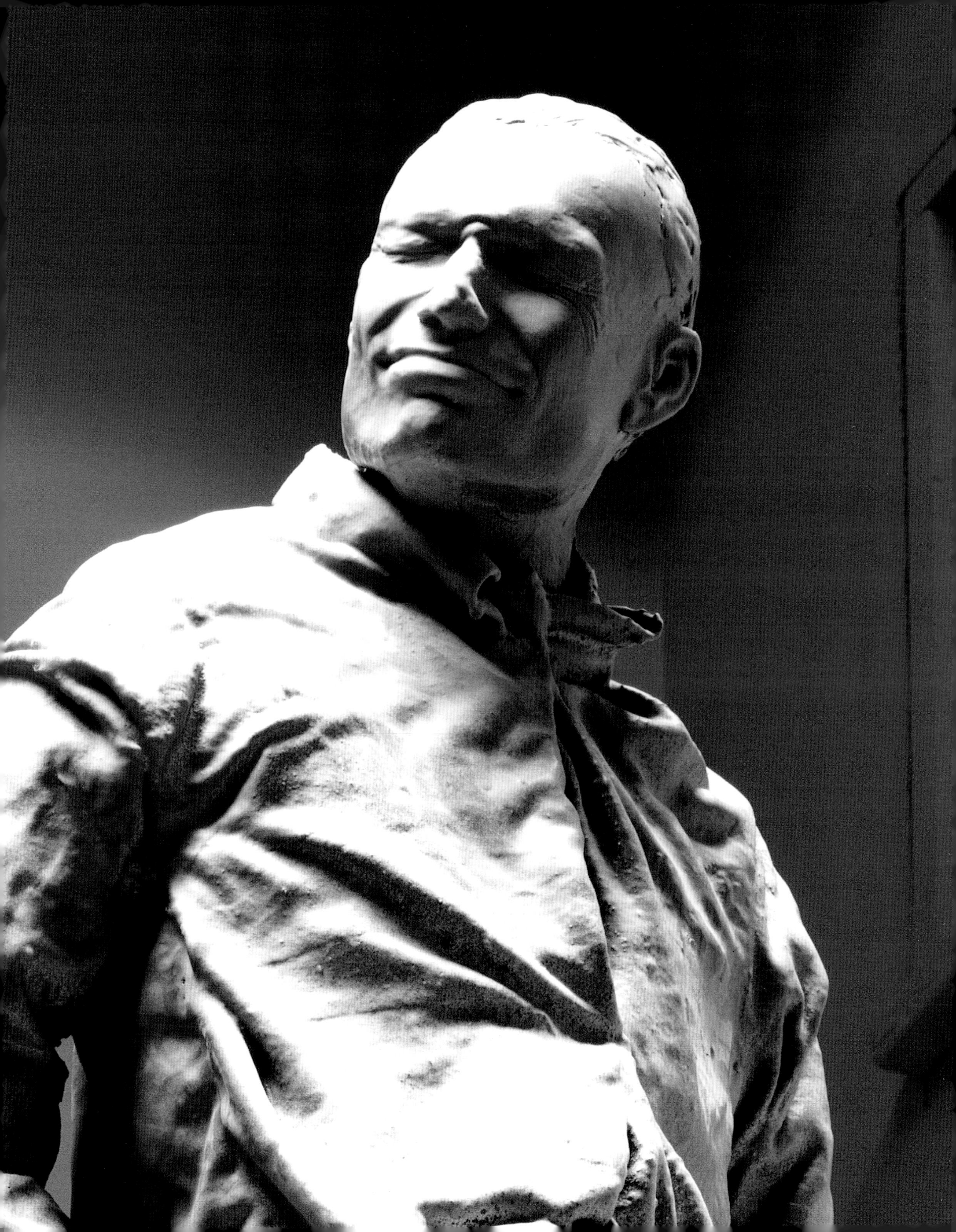

Chronology

1953 Born in Madrid

1976–7 Central School of Art and Design, London

1978–80 Croydon School of Art, London

1981–2 Pratt Graphic Center, New York

Lives and works in Madrid

AWARDS

1978–80 British Council scholarship for Advanced Printmaking, Croydon School of Art, London

1981–2 Fullbright Fellowship, North American Spanish Committee for Pratt Graphic Center, New York

1996 *Will it be a Likeness?* by John Berger and Juan Muñoz wins 'Hörspiel des Jahres 1996' for the best radio programme in Germany

2000 Awarded the 'Premio Nacional de Bellas Artes', Spain

1984 *Últimos Trabajos*, Galería Fernando Vijande, Madrid*

1985 *Retrato de um homem em pé de Pontorno*, Galeria Cómicos, Lisbon

1986 Galerie Joost Declercq, Ghent
Galería Marga Paz, Madrid

1987 Galerie Roger Pailhas, Marseille
Sculptures de 1985 à 1987, CAPC Musée d'Art Contemporain, Bordeaux
Lisson Gallery, London
Estudos para a descrição de um lugar, Galeria Cómicos, Lisbon

1988 Galerie Jean Bernier, Athens
Galerie Konrad Fischer, Düsseldorf
Galerie Ghislaine Hussenot, Paris

1989 *A Room For A Doctor of Pain*, a project with Paul Robbrecht, Galería Marga Paz, Madrid
Galerie Joost Declercq, Ghent
Lisson Gallery, London
Galería Marga Paz, Madrid

1990 Galerie Jean Bernier, Athens
Segment, The Renaissance Society, Chicago and Centre d'Art Contemporain, Geneva*
Arnolfini Gallery, Bristol

1991 Galerie Konrad Fischer, Dusseldorf
Arbeiten 1988 bis 1990, Museum Haus Lange, Krefeld*
Marian Goodman Gallery, New York
Sculpturen, Stedelijk van Abbemuseum, Eindhoven
Galerie Ghislaine Hussenot, Paris

1992 *Conversaciones*, Centro del Carme, Instituto Valenciano de Arte Moderno, Valencia*
Drawings & Prints, Frith Street Gallery, London

1993 Marian Goodman Gallery, New York
Galerie Jean Bernier, Athens
Lisson Gallery, London
Galerie Konrad Fischer, Dusseldorf

1994 Carré d'Art – Musée d'Art Contemporain, Nimes*
Juan Muñoz: Sculpture, Drawings and Installation, The Irish Museum of Modern Art, Dublin*

1995 *A Portrait of a Turkish Man Drawing*, Isabella Stuart Gardner Museum, Boston*
Centro Galego de Arte Contemporáneo, Santiago de Compostela
Kunstverein Hamburg, Hamburg

1996 *A Place Called Abroad*, Dia Center for the Arts, New York*
Monólogos y diálogos, Palacio de Velázquez, Museo Nacional Centro de Arte Reina Sofia, Madrid*

1997 *Directions*, Hirshhorn Museum and Sculpture Garden, Washington DC
Galleria Continua, San Gimignano
Galerie Chislaine Hussenot, Paris
Monologe und Dialoge, Museum für Gegenwartskunst, Zürich*

1998 *Certain drawings in oil and ink 1996–1998*, Sala Robayera, Miengo*

1999 *Crossroads*, Marian Goodman Gallery, New York
A brief description of my death, Bernier & Eliades Gallery, Athens

2000 *The Nature of Visual Illusion*, Lousiana Museum of Modern Art, Copenhagen

2001 *Double Bind*, Tate Modern, London

2001 Hirshhorn Museum and Sculpture Garden, Washington DC. Touring until 2003 to: Museum of Contemporary Art, Los Angeles; The Art Institute of Chicago; Contemporary Arts Museum, Houston

* associated catalogue or publication

1981   Fri-art 81, Fribourg*

1982   Büro Berlin, Berlin*

1983   *La Imagen del Animal: arte prehistórico, arte
contemporáneo*, Caja de Ahorros y Monte
de Piedad, Casa del Monte, Palacio de
las Alhajas, Madrid

1985   Stedelijk van Abbemuseum, Eindhoven*

1986   *Chambres d'Amis*, Museum van
Hedendaagse Kunst, Ghent*
Aperto 86, Cuatro Artistas Españoles,
XLII Biennale di Venezia*

1987   *Espagne 87: Dynamiques et Interrogations*,
ARC – Musée d'Art Moderne de la Ville,
Paris*

1988   *Steirischer Herbst '88*, Grazer Kunstverein,
Stadtmuseum Graz*

1989   *Magiciens de la terre*, Musée National d'Art
Moderne, Centre Georges Pompidou et
La Grande Halle de la Villette, Paris*
*Theatergarden Bestiarium: The garden as
theater as museum*, PS1, Long Island City,
New York*
Spanish Art Today, The Museum of
Modern Art, Takanawa, Karuizawa*

1990   *OBJECTives: The new sculptures*,
Newport Harbour Art Museum,
Newport Beach*
*The Readymade Boomerang: Certain
relations in 20th-century art*, The Eighth
Biennale of Sydney, Art Gallery of
New South Wales, Australia*
Possible Worlds, Sculpture from Europe,
Serpentine Gallery and Institute of
Contemporary Arts, London*

1991   *Metropolis: International Art Exhibition*,
Martin-Gropius-Bau, Berlin*
Trans/Mission: Art in Intercultural Limbo,
Rooseum Center for Contemporary Art,
Malmo, Sweden*
Carnegie International 1991, The Carnegie
Museum of Art, Pittsburgh,
Pennsylvania*

1992   *Doubletake: Collective Memory and Current
Art*, Southbank Centre Hayward Gallery,
London and Kunsthalle Wien*
Documenta IX, Museum Fridericianum,
Kassel*
The Boundary Rider, 9th Biennale of
Sydney*

1993   *Sonsbeek '93*, Arnhem, The Netherlands*
*The Sublime Void: On the memory of the
imagination*, Antwerp '93, Koninklijk,
Museum voor Schone Kunsten,
Antwerp*

1994   *Welt-Moral: Moralvorstellungen in der Kunst
heute*, Kunsthalle Basel*

1995   *Private/Public*, Ars 95, Nykytaiteen Museo
– Valtion Taidemuseo, Helsinki*
Ripple Across the Water, The Watari
Museum of Contemporary Art, Tokyo*

1996   *City Space 1996*, Sculptures and
installations made for Copenhagen 96,
Copenhagen*
Marks: Artists work throughout Jerusalem,
The Israel Museum, Jerusalem*

1997   La Biennale di Venezia: XLVII
Esposizione internationale d'arte,
Venice*
L'Autre: 4th Biennale d'art contemporain
de Lyon, Musée d'Art Contemporain,
Lyon*

1998   *Voice Over: Sound and vision in current art*,
Arnolfini Gallery, Bristol*
*Wounds between democracy and redemption
in contemporary art*, Moderna Museet,
Stockholm*

1999   *The Passion and the Wave*, 6th International
Istanbul Biennial, Istanbul*
Trace, Liverpool Biennial of
Contemporary Art, Tate Gallery,
Liverpool*

2000   *Over the Edges*, Stedelijk Museum voor
Actuele Kunst, Gent*
Biennale of Sydney 2000, 12th Biennale
of Sydney*
Around 1984: A Look at Art in the 80s, P.S.1,
Long Island City, New York*
Between Cinema and a Hard Place,
Tate Modern, London

2001   *Collaborations with Parkett; 1984 to Now*,
The Museum of Modern Art, New York
*A Contemporary Cabinet of Curiosities:
Selections of the Logan Collection*, California
College of Arts and Crafts Institute*

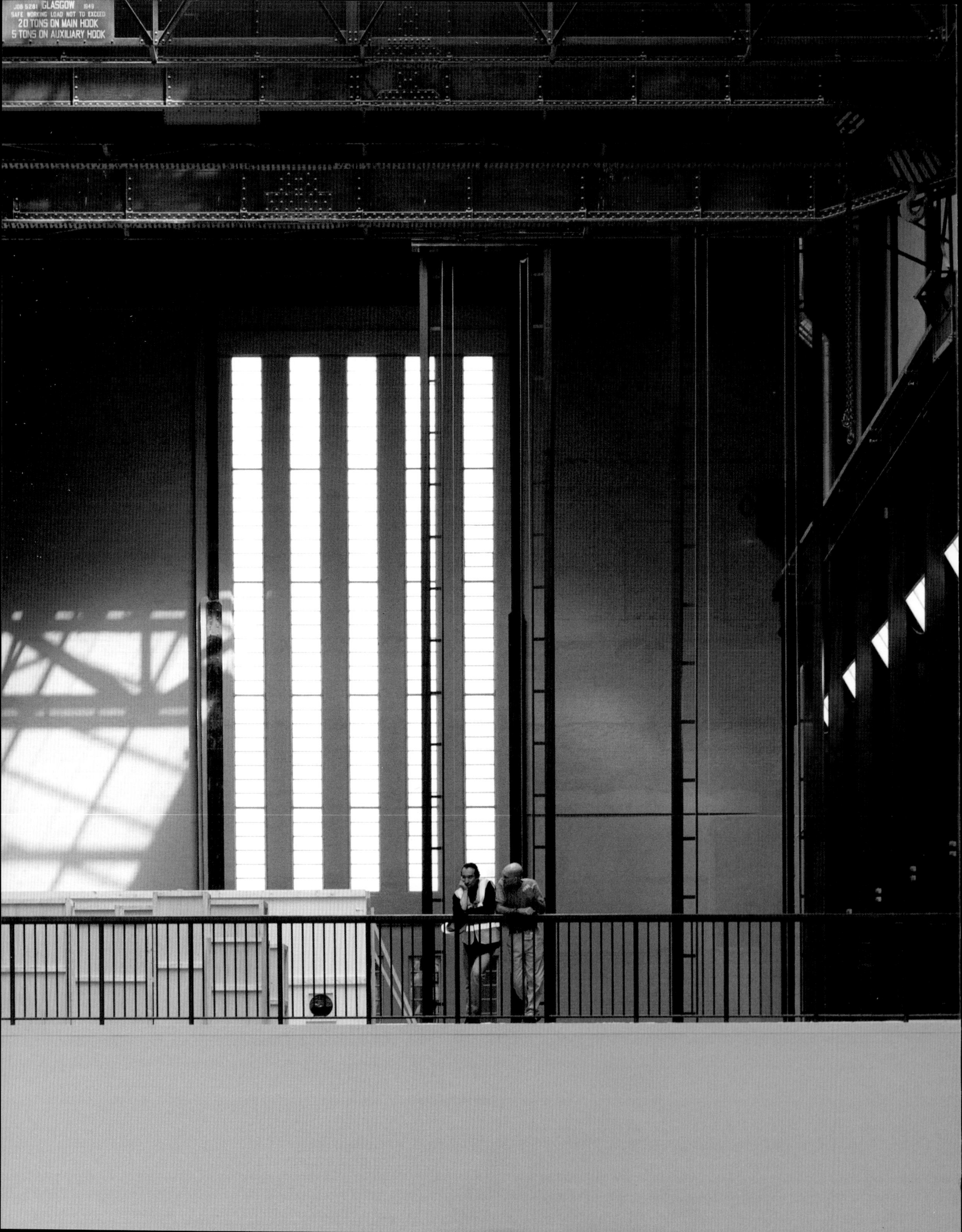

JOB 5281 GLASGOW 1949
SAFE WORKING LOAD NOT TO EXCEED
20 TONS ON MAIN HOOK
5 TONS ON AUXILIARY HOOK

Acknowledgements

She was the first person I met, and she was the last one when I left.
I would like to thank Susan May, for she saw how the first Rorschach ink-blot
became this ambiguous story.

Between the seer and the subject of the gaze there is a gap.
James Lingwood has helped me once again to make visible that narrow space.

Victor Alarcón, Herminia Muñoz and Rubén Polanco brought me their friendship.

David Scholefield brought along Neil Thomas, who brought David Mason, who
brought Dennis Reason. Andrew McAlpine brought Jim Morahan. Anthony Joseph
brought Peter McKinnon, who brought Belinda Clisham and Anna Stamper.
John Johnson came with his friends. Alone they came: Deklan Kilfeather,
Jesse Ash, Barry Hobson.

Philip Lewis and Attilio Maranzano brought their vision to this catalogue.

JUAN MUÑOZ

COPYRIGHT CREDITS
Works of art © Juan Muñoz 2001
Photographs of *Gatherings*
(pp.6–7, 10–11, 13–56, 120) © Tate 2001
Photographs of *Double Bind* (pp.79–116)
© Attilio Maranzano 2001

PHOTOGRAPHIC CREDITS
The drawings, photographs and
texts in *Gatherings* (pp.13–56)
were collected and compiled by
Juan Muñoz between 20 March 2000
and 3 June 2001, and photographed
for this book by Rod Tidnam of
Tate Photography

COVER *Double Bind* 2001
PHOTO Attilio Maranzano

FRONTISPIECE The Turbine Hall,
Tate Modern
PHOTO Juan Muñoz

Published by order of the Tate
Trustees 2001 on the occasion of
the exhibition at Tate Modern,
London, 12 June 2001 to
10 February 2002

ISBN 1 85437 358 7

A catalogue record for this
publication is available from
the British Library

Published by Tate Publishing,
a division of Tate Enterprises Ltd
Millbank
London SW1P 4RG

'A Conversation, May 2001'
© James Lingwood 2001

Designed and typeset by
Philip Lewis at LewisHallam,
London

Printed and bound in
Great Britain by BAS Printers,
Over Wallop, Hampshire

This exhibition is the
second commission in
The Unilever Series

Juan Muñoz and David Scholefield, May 2001

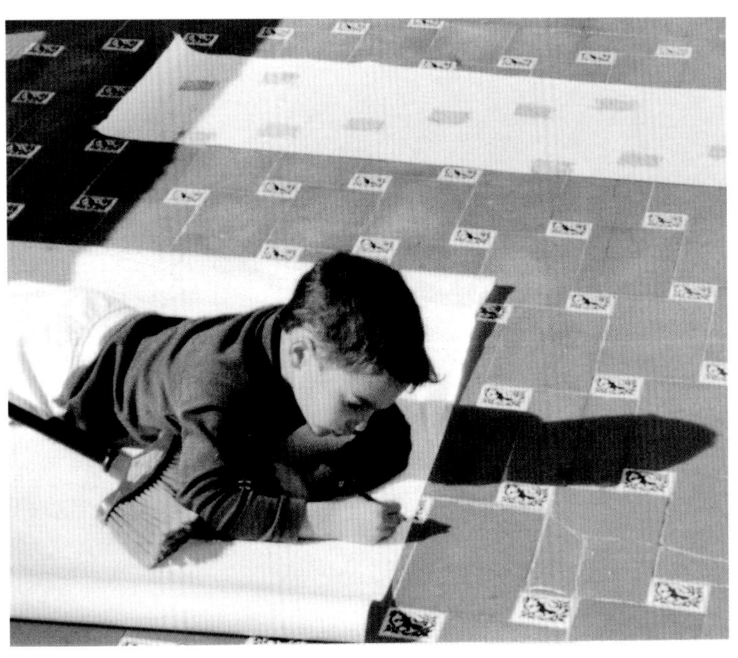